FOUL DEEDS & SUSPICIOUS DEATHS
IN DUBLIN

Foul Deeds and Suspicious Deaths in

DUBLIN

Stephen Wade

Wharncliffe Books

This book is for Daisy Cummins

First published in Great Britain in 2008 by
Wharncliffe Books
an imprint of
Pen & Sword Books Ltd
47 Church Street
Barnsley
South Yorkshire
S70 2AS

ISBN: 978 184563 067 6

A CIP catalogue record for this book is available from
the British Library

Typeset in Plantin and ITC Benguiat by
Mousemat Design Limited

Printed and bound in Great Britain by CPI UK

Pen & Sword Books Ltd incorporates the imprints of
Pen & Sword Aviation, Pen & Sword Maritime,
Pen & Sword Military, Wharncliffe Local History,
Pen and Sword Select, Pen and Sword Military Classics
and Leo Cooper.

For a complete list of Pen & Sword titles please contact
PEN & SWORD BOOKS LIMITED
47 Church Street, Barnsley, South Yorkshire,
S70 2AS, England
E-mail: enquiries@pen-and-sword.co.uk
Website: www.pen-and-sword.co.uk

Contents

Acknowledgements

There are many people and institutions to thank for their help in making this book possible. In terms of helping with illustrations and sources, I have to thank the National Library of Ireland. The images 'Man walking on Eden Quay' by J J Clarke and the two images 'The Alarm Clock of Labour' and 'Irish Worker of 1925' are reproduced courtesy of the National Library of Ireland. My attempts to have some help in the use of images from the 'last dying speeches ' proved fruitless at Trinity College. But staff at the National Museum of Ireland were very helpful and kind.

For help with finding some sources, I have to thank Daisy Cummins, my Dublin correspondent. For the wider story, the metanarrative of Ireland, the masters Roy Foster, Robert Kee and Cecil Woodham-Smith and their writings stand firmly behind all these tales, as touchstones. For help in understanding the complexities of the 1913 Lock-out, the magisterial work, *Disturbed Dublin* by Arnold Wright, was invaluable. For the pictures of the Larkin chapter I have to thank the National Library of Ireland, in particular, Gerry Kavanagh. Sean Murphy's writings helped a great deal with the crown jewels story.

Particular useful in secondary sources have been Frank Hopkins' wonderful *Rare Old Dublin* (see bibliography) and for Mountjoy, Tim Carey and his book, *Mountjoy: Story of a Prison* and Maggie Murphy's *My Experience of Prison: Mountjoy* (1912). For some oral history, thanks to Pat Larkin, Daisy Cummins, Kate Walker and in that respect, I owe a great deal to the historian of Monto, Terry Fagan and Sergeant Robert Burke.

My editor, Brian Elliott, is as always, the main support in the telling of 'Foul Deeds'.

Introduction

For all kinds of complex reasons, the city of Dublin has, throughout history, attracted a great deal of bad press in the media with regard to crime. In recent years there have been newspaper features about the 'drug capital' underworld nature of the city. The press always want to highlight negative elements, of course, but certainly in earlier times, Dublin crime rates were higher than the major British cities. The reasons for that are not hard to find. Poverty in some areas of the city in late Victorian years was marked by widespread deprivation and ill health in the population. Poverty is always a next-door neighbour to crime.

In 1911, the Recorder of Dublin gave an address to the Grand Jury at the City Sessions and said that there were 123 bills for them to listen to from ninety-two district cases; of these, thirteen were for riot and disorder and eleven for serious assault and intimidation 'arising from the industrial disturbances which had prevailed in the city'. But he took time to explain the severe problems in the tenements: speaking of the housing of the poor, he said that the 'costliness of disease and intemperance, in which much of the crime in Dublin originated, should enforce attention to the subject of providing wholesome houses'. He gave some stunning figures: the rate of mortality when the corporation bought the old houses averaged 50 per thousand in a year. Four per thousand deaths were from 'phthisis' (tuberculosis). Everything in his words pointed to extreme poverty, and so desperate crime was rife in some areas.

But the city has a history of paradoxes: the centre of the Irish Literary Renaissance led by W B Yeats and Douglas Hyde, and yet a place where riot and disorder were part of life for centuries. After all, the place has been the scene of many rebellions and battles that an intransigent nature settled and somehow gathered a creative spin-off into the arts.

Consequently the crime and lawlessness sat uneasily alongside the incredible literary and artistic flowering of Dublin. The city can claim great writers by the handful: Oscar Wilde, James Joyce, Sean O'Casey, Bernard Shaw, Brendan Behan and many others.

Dublin has been Norse, Celtic, British and Norman. Its sense of identity has always been one concerned with divisions. The crime associated with the place had therefore always bordered on either politics in a broad sense, or with power more apparent 'on the doorstep' of everyday life. Hence my chapters include duels, riots, strikes and robberies. What the book does not include, with one exception, is the violence related to the political struggles for independence; I consider that to be well accounted for in thousands of books easily available. With the exception of the war crime which was a murder - that of Sheehy Skeffington – this book is concerned with such offences as homicide, theft, public disorder, libel and fraud. Some stories are grand, part of the sweep of history, such as the 'Liberty Boys' and some are those typical domestic tragedies taking place when things go seriously wrong in relationships and families. But what provides a constant backdrop to the crimes is a turbulent social history across the timeline of the book, from the mid-seventeenth century to the 1960s. The population of the city in 1900 was over 400,000, and the fact of a massive population in a limited urban space is bedrock to all kinds of clashes, confrontations and grievances, so Dublin crime has often been visible, street-focused crime. Back in 1790, the *Hibernian* magazine put the blame clearly on the English:

> *Dublin at this moment swarms with a flight of English sharpers – adepts at the mysteries of their profession, and general professors in the arts of shop-lifting, pocket-picking, ring-dropping, swindling and coining. They assume all shapes and appearances – clergymen, farmers, horse-jockeys, agents…. . And are straight or deformed, young or old, lame or otherwise just as occasion suits.*

There are also places in the city which resonate to the low, sad sound of death and suffering: the prisons. The very words Mountjoy and Kilmainham send a shiver through history. But there have been others, smaller gaols such as Newgate in the old Corn Market, and the 'Black Dog' (the Sheriff's Marshalsea) and the Four Courts Marshalsea off Thomas Street. There was also the New Prison, built on Little Green. They all had their stories and scandals and they provide a part of the foundation for the stories here recalled. In 1729, the Irish House of Commons set up an inquiry into the condition of the city's gaols, and among other problems they discovered that the keeper of the Black Dog was doing very well with a sideline business of 'vending liquor to the prisoners' and he also forced money out of all clients. Anyone who would not pay was stripped and beaten.

The Richmond bridewell closed in 1887 and Mountjoy after that became more important and prominent. After 1897, female convicts were placed there also, after the closure of Grangegorman Female Penitentiary. Kilmainham and Mountjoy together averaged around 10,000 prisoners each year from across the country.

The other dominant presence behind many stories is Dublin Castle, scene of so many key moments in Irish history, and a symbol of the contradictions and paradoxes which create the Dublin of times past: a place where there have been balls and parties, speeches and meetings, yet also imprisonment and torments; a place of grandeur yet a scene of fear and alien power. The ghosts of rebels and fighters surely hang around the walls, as it has seen many heads impaled on spikes. As Richard Stanyhurst wrote:

> *These trunkless heads do plainly show*
> *Each rebel's fatal end.*
> *And what a heinous crime it is*
> *The Queen for to offend.*

Another feature of the city's legal and organisational history is the police presence, and in addition to the trouble caused by the very military police force established in 1786, the Dublin Metropolitan Police had a very busy time in Victorian years. In the years between 1870 and 1894 half of all the major crimes committed in Ireland fell at their door. Dublin was well ahead of the rest of the land in the crime statistic, however. In 1910, there were 852 indictable offences in Dublin, compared with 541 in Belfast and 215 in Cork. Total offences for Dublin in that year came to 9,021, compared to 5,938 in Belfast and 5,178 in Cork.

Some of the following stories are not violent or in any way horrible and black tales of terrible suffering. 'Foul deeds' may be far more subtle. Included here are the bizarre cases of Sir William Wilde being tormented by a serial libel accuser, a fight at the opening of the contentious play, *The Playboy of the Western World*, by John Synge, and the antics of some wild apprentices. It would have been too easy, but also more monotonous, simply to build the narratives around the catalogue of hangings.

Of the earlier crimes, the stories have been easier to assemble thanks to James Kelly's book, *Gallows Speeches* (see bibliography) and for details of the executioner Pierrepoint's visits to ply his trade across the Irish Sea, thanks go to the work of Steve Fielding, specialist historian of the noose and scaffold. Otherwise, many of the sources have been from ephemera, and some put together from scattered memoirs and anecdotes. Crime stories do not always have a satisfying resolution, but they certainly should have drama and sensation, and these stories have those elements in abundance.

CHAPTER 1

Highwaymen and Robbers
1640

'. . . he issued his own laws, levied tolls on pedlars, he was Captain
General of the Irish robbers . . .'
LIVES AND ADVENTURES OF THE MOST NOTORIOUS
IRISH HIGHWAYMEN

A soon as the eye chances on a reference to 'highwaymen' we think of Robin Hood and Dick Turpin, and legend takes over from the history. Turpin, for all the Victorian glorification, murdered and raped; there was no glamour there, and the same may be said of Ireland's 'gentlemen of the road' who were in fact, no gentlemen at all. They were heartless rogues out for survival at first and then later for wealth, profit and the thrill of tormenting victims.

Ireland, along with every other country with a rich folklore, has its share of tales from that distant past in which truth is shrouded in myth and legend. There is a long and rich tradition of oral storytelling in Irish culture, of course, and also a good store of texts from popular street literature such as last dying speeches and hanging narratives. But among those old tales, few themes are as attractive and enduring as stories of highwaymen.

The Dick Turpin figure in Irish history is undoubtedly Redmond O'Hanlon, probably born around 1620 in County Armagh. As a soldier,

Dick Turpin, from an old print. Author's collection

he fought with the Irish Catholic rebel army under Owen Roe O'Neill at the battle of Benburb in 1646. After various adventures across Europe he came home and learned that he had lost his land and inheritance, so he took to the road. The truth about him appears to be that, far from being a romantic figure, he was capable of extorting money for protection and of putting the fear of God into anyone who opposed him.

In Dublin, at the time when O'Hanlon was about fifty years old, the authorities were out to get him and there were posters around the town offering a reward to anyone with information that would lead to his capture. The militia were out to find him, but it seems that he had a tough and numerous gang with him

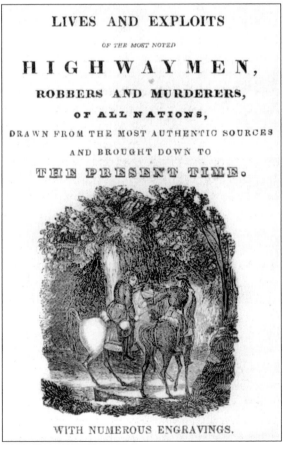

Frontispiece from The Lives and exploits of the noted Highwaymen *1825.*

Author's collection

and it would have taken a considerable force of men to take him. The turning point, something that spurred the authorities to more determined attitudes and actions, was the murder of James Butler, Duke of Ormonde, in 1679. But, as with many tales of past villains, his downfall came from his own kin, his brother killing him in his sleep. This was near Hilltown, County Armagh, in 1681.

His myth persisted, particularly with the publication of William Carleton's novel, *The Irish Repparee*, in 1862. But there is little of myth in the sordid and thoroughly nasty life of a more earthy and unscrupulous thug, Patrick Flemming, who figures in the celebrated *Newgate Calendar* and in the Old Bailey records. Flemming was one of Dublin's worst rogues in the seventeenth century who, after an assortment of crimes in Dublin, began a reign of terror in the Bog of Allen.

Flemming, like O'Hanlon, began his working life in the service of the nobility, being a foot-boy with the household of the Countess of Kildare. The rebellious spirit was in him from early on, and he was reported to grow 'not only careless but insolent' and he was discharged. After that he managed to find some work at the home of the Earl of Antrim, and after becoming totally unmanageable, he was told to go, but according to his biography after his execution, Flemming '... found means, before he left the neighbourhood, to rob his lordship of money and plate to the value of two hundred pounds, with which he fled to Athenry...'.

After hiding out for a while, he decided to go to Dublin and there he joined a gang on the streets, housebreaking. The Old Bailey record says that in six years in Dublin he was 'concerned in more robberies than had ever before been committed in that city in the memory of man'. In Dublin, he was very close to being hanged on a few occasions, and it looked as though his destiny would be the gibbet on Stephen's Green. But he left town and moved to the place that would be forever linked to his name – the Bog of Allen.

There, he became the most feared robber of his age, willing to prey upon anyone, regardless of their status or power. He even robbed people such as the Archbishop of Armagh and the Bishop of Rapho. His biographer was fond of exaggeration, we have to say, because the claim was that Flemming, in just a few

Cover of Highway Robbery Under Arms *by a notorious Dubliner.* Author's collection

days, 'robbed one hundred and twenty five men and women upon the mountain of Barnsmoor'. That was apparently his den where the gang assembled. After a kidnapping and blackmail campaign, he left the area and did the same reign of terror in Munster.

The story was that he was captured and put in a country gaol but then smashed his way to freedom. But fate caught up with him and he was taken at a house near Mancoth. There, the landlord turned informer (in true Billy the Kid tradition) and the law arrived.

Flemming was hanged in Dublin on 24 April 1650. His body suffered the indignity of being hanged in chains, as with the English gibbet tradition, for birds to peck at and for other aspiring villains to see and shudder at, on a public road not far from town. Some said that the landlord who informed on him even wet all the firearms of Flemming and his gang.

The course of his career is entirely typical, with all the elements of a good story told around the fire from the oral tradition. One of the distinctive features is the fact that he was betrayed by someone who knew him. That he was the king of his own little patch of ground, making people pay tolls to pass, is entirely in keeping with the Robin Hood and the O'Hanlon tales.

But the Dublin highwaymen do not stop in the seventeenth and eighteenth centuries: the tradition went on in the Australian bushrangers, where one of the most infamous, a Dubliner called Jack Bradshaw, taken from Dublin to Melbourne by a relative; and there, when he grew up, highway robbery became his trade. The title of his autobiography says it all: *Highway Robbery Under Arms without Shedding Blood.* Of course, as with all these misguided heroes of popular tales, the truth is that they were often locked away, as Bradshaw's sub-title says: 'Twenty years of Prison Life in the Gaols of New South Wales.'

CHAPTER 2

An Abominable Sin

1640

'My whole life seems ruined by this man.
The tower of ivory is assailed by the foul thing . . .'
OSCAR WILDE

Oscar Wilde's words in a letter to 'Bosie' were written 300 years after the subject of this chapter, Bishop John Atherton, was in serious trouble for alleged sodomy. But the words in Wilde's letter could easily apply. One man brought down the Bishop, starting with one accusation of serious misconduct and then the house of cards, that was the Bishop's life, came down.

But our story begins with a ghost story, told at great length recently by Peter Marshall, who has researched Atherton's story in depth. When Susan Leakey of Minehead died, she supposedly returned in spirit to disturb all kinds of good Somerset people. Her son-in-law, John Atherton, was to feel the after-shocks of that when he progressed in his church career. He married Susan's daughter, started out as vicar of the village of Huish Champflower, and then became Bishop of Waterford and Lismore from 1636 to his death in 1640.

It is a long and complex tale, but it ended in Dublin with the

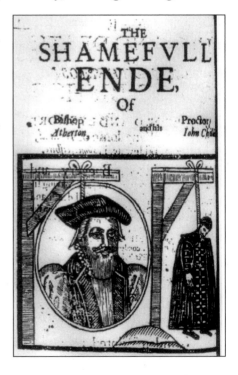

Atherton in a contemporary chapbook.
Author's collection

Bishop at the end of a rope. In the first part of the tale, when Susan 'Mother' Leakey began to appear in apparition and the society around Minehead was stirred up. At a time when such things were more often linked to demonic than to Christian notions by Protestants, it was a phenomenon that attracted interest in the higher echelons of the church. Catholics would have had no problem as they believe in purgatory of course. But in the seventeenth century when witchcraft was a dark art in need of severe punishment in the eyes of many, Minehead and its doings were seen by some powerful people as possibly the centre of some evil doings.

But for John Atherton, there was a way of escape. There had always been strong links between Somerset coastal towns (and indeed Bristol) and Dublin, with both trade and piracy being common over the centuries. But Atherton was fortunate in having Irish links at a time when the Earl of Strafford, Thomas Wentworth, became Lord Deputy of Ireland, and he had caught the eye of some powerful clerics. Preferment came his way and he was placed in Lismore for the centre of his Bishopric.

Atherton, initially related to Strafford's star on the rise, would have seen Wentworth, when he was sent to govern Ireland in 1633, become a tyrant, and he must have seen that what was to become known as the 'Bishops' Wars'. When he was impeached for alienating the King's subjects, matters were grim and he had to defend himself with his life at stake. At that point, Atherton was already dead, an early casualty of the 'wars'.

Strafford was executed on Tower Hill a year after Atherton had been hanged in Dublin. Atherton's downfall started with an accusation from his steward, John Child. Child claimed that he had indulged in sodomy with him – and that was a felony and a capital offence in 1640. Almost a century before, in 1533, parliament had made the 'abominable vice of buggery' into a capital offence. Then, in contrast, in Ireland it had only been a hanging offence for six years at the time of Atherton's trial. It was also bad luck for Atherton in that just a few years before Child's accusations, there had been a high profile case of sodomy against a nobleman, the Earl of Castlehaven. The crime was in England, but the Earl, Mervyn Touchet, had his title from Ireland.

It all began when Child, who would be committing a felony himself if the accusation were proved, so the implication had to be that he was telling the truth, unless he was totally out of his senses. Just to make that accusation publicly was a confession about one's own offence. Child made a petition and that was presented to parliament and the man who was then in place as the new Lord Deputy, Sir Christopher Wandesford, who announced that what he found in the petition would make all men blush when they saw 'what stuff was in it'.

As for John Atherton, he planned to attend what would be his last service at Christ Church cathedral, and he did not exactly hide away in a corner, because he was noted to be dressed in all his fine ecclesiastic attire. But Wandesford, perhaps fearing open trouble did not allow him to go. Clearly, there was a great deal of embarrassment in the men of the cloth in the midst of all this 'bad press' for the church. Other enemies of Atherton came out of the woodwork and joined in the attack. One of these was the steward to the Earl of Cork, John Walley, who delighted in taking the opportunity to gather all kinds of other scraps of evidence against the Bishop. In one of his letters he wrote that the Bishop of Waterford had been found out and 'his filthy and odious sins of sodomy and adultery laid open to the world'.

Tongues wagged across England as well as Ireland and other men set about laying into Atherton. One of these was a scandal-monger, Edmund Rossingham, who told anyone who came across his pamphlet that Atherton had been accused by a servant of his being buggered by the Bishop. He added that many other charges had accumulated, and these he described as 'many other

Christ Church where the Bishop last appeared. The Graphic

foul offences' which were 'adulteries and single fornications'.

The Bishop was arrested in June 1640 and a number of other men were charged and imprisoned following Child's letter. Atherton's career in the church was over, even if he escaped

St Stephen's Green Memorial. Hangings took place here during the eighteenth century. The author

conviction. The dirt-digging carried on, and someone searched the man's past, back in Minehead. What happened was that a researcher found that the Bishop had committed incest because he had married the sister of his wife. That was regarded as incest at that time. But to make things worse, the ghost of Susan Leakey, known as 'Mother Leakey' had been alleged to have said rather cryptic things, including the statement that a religious man there had been 'vomited out to Ireland'.

Atherton was tried at the King's Bench court in Dublin Castle but unfortunately, the records of the trial were destroyed in 1641 when there was a general rebellion across the land. But fortunately for the historian, felons about to die were in the practice of making last dying speeches (see Chapter 4) and Atherton did so. He had had to put forward his own defence as he had not been allowed a lawyer; he had prepared a detailed written defence for himself after researching in reference works. But things were extremely severe for him because there had also been a charge of rape. A certain John Price saw Atherton die, and he knew something of the trial, saying that Atherton had had to answer sodomy and rape charges; it seems that a surprise witness, a young boy, had given evidence which almost certainly condemned Atherton. He was found guilty on the two capital charges.

One small detail on the day of his execution gave one consolation in terms of posterity, yet it meant nothing. That was the fact that he was still technically a Bishop when he died. The Board of Trinity College took away his doctorate on the morning on which he was to die, but Sir Christopher Wandesford died that morning so there had been no signature to enact that measure. Atherton died a bishop and, as Peter Marshall has noted, he was the only Anglican prelate 'to have been convicted and executed for the crime of sodomy'.

As Atherton walked up the ladder on Stephen's Green he said: 'I thank God, I dread not death.' But even in his last words there is dispute. One witness said his last words were:

I do here before the Lord, his holy angels and you all, own the Sentence against me to die this manner of death be just, and I was Guilty of the charge laid against me.

But another man said that Atherton denied the crime. On 12

May 1641, Thomas Wentworth, Earl of Strafford, also died for his supposed crimes, and he was beheaded, an exit from this life considered to be more swift and merciful. It was with a good, skilled axeman and no doubt Wentworth parted with some money to ask for that last favour.

A poem of the time has this to say of Atherton:

> *He surely warned was to mend his life,*
> *By his own sister, Master Leakey's wife,*
> *And in her lifetime conscious how he led*
> *His lustful life, her ghost in ghastful wise*
> *Did oft appear before her sister's eyes.*

And the ghost said: 'Daughter, 'tis the wicked life your brother leads, warn him to mend his life.'

It seems that she did, but to no effect.

CHAPTER 3

Sham Speeches: Charles Donnell
1712

*'Depend upon it Sir, when a man knows he is to be hanged in
a fortnight, it concentrates the mind wonderfully.'*
SAMUEL JOHNSON

A convicted killer in 1712 in Dublin tried everything he could to save his life. There was even a signed statement by his father-in-law concerning his morals; Thomas Pullman of Capel Street wrote: '... ever since the said Charles was married to the deponent's daughter he never assaulted, beat or abused this deponent or this deponent's wife, as has been scandalously reported. This deponent further deposeth that since the said Charles has been confined in Newgate, he never was unthankful for any victuals sent to him from this deponent's house..' It would be difficult to find anything more desperate than that, from a condemned man. His luck never changed for the better, either, and it does look as though he had enemies who wanted him gone, maybe people with scores to settle, for the man in question lived a life of violence and antagonism.

Charles Donnell was born in Ballymena, Antrim, but after going his own way in life and running into all kinds of trouble, his father decided that the best idea for the wayward son was to send him off to sea, so he was bound apprentice to a Dublin seaman, Captain Robert Macarroll. But after a trip to Virginia which was full of difficulties, he drifted home. He married Mrs Esther Pullman in Dublin, after cutting himself off from his family. From that point, he had grand plans, mainly the notion of going back home, but fate stepped in. He took the life of another man.

We know from his last dying speech spoken near Stephen's Green on 8 November 1712, that he was, as expected, contrite and bursting with regret and self-reproach:

The Memorial Park in Green Street where Newgate stood. The author

My dear father's inclinations were that I should follow my study as my brothers had done; but to my great sorrow and grief, I did not observe his paternal and good advice in that, and many other occurrences of my life… let me advise and admonish all young unthinking men, to be obedient to their parents…

What happened to Donnell happened to hundreds of wild rakes around the city: he was, as he puts it 'overtaken with drink', and he said that he had no knowledge of the fact that he had killed a man: 'I do not remember how that unhappy accident happened betwixt me and that unfortunate gentleman Mr Britton, who lost his life.' In other words, it was a drunken fight. All he could say in his statement was that he knew both he and Britton had their swords drawn, so Donnell was looking to his Counsel to help him evade the date with the hangman by arguing that the death of Britton, rather than being murder, premeditated, was a lesser case of what could be called 'chance medley' – a type of what was later manslaughter.

Chance medley was, as it is defined in the Old Bailey Session Papers, a verdict used in murder cases where the killing did not involve premeditated malice but it was thought that the killer was at least partially at fault. But in the eighteenth century it was a verdict used inconsistently. It had tended to be used most commonly in accidental deaths such as a person being run over by a cart or being accidentally shot.

A more promising defence for a man who had taken a life in a drunken brawl was from an act of 1604, and Donnell refers to this in his statement: 'The trial came on, and there being two indictments against me, one for murder and the other upon the statute of stabbing, I was found guilty at large.' The 'statute of stabbing' said that 'if anyone stabs another, who hath not at that time drawn a weapon, or hath not first stricken, the party who stabs is deemed guilty of murder, if the person stabbed dies within six months afterwards.' That statute had condemned Deborah Churchill, for instance, just four years before Donnell, in London. She had intervened in a fight between a man and her lover, and her intervention, distracting her lover's opponent resulted in the opponent's death. She was arraigned and charged as an accomplice and hanged at Tyburn.

The last journey, from an old print. Author's collection

Donnell was acquitted of the stabbing as there was proof that the other man was armed, but there was a certain level of legal wrangling and strategy regarding the charge of murder, and he lost the case. His explanation was that his friends were arguing for a sentence of transportation, but there was an error made by the jury and, had he known at the time, he could have had grounds for what was called an arrest of judgement. But his Counsel clearly told him not to offend: as he said he acted in 'fear of incensing the court, which already seemed inclined to mercy, more especially when my friends moved only for transportation'.

The arrest of judgement is the point of law which allows for an accused to prevent the judgement and sentence because of a technical defect in the indictment. That appears to stem from the fault of there being the second indictment, something without grounds.

The unfortunate Donnell was trying to explain, in his last dying speech, that he may have escaped the noose had he been better advised. He ended that speech with an invective against false friends – and there had been a desperate attempt to obtain a pardon. His brother Robert, a clergyman, had gone to London to work for a pardon and had written to Charles with encouraging news, but Charles claimed that 'many scandalous stories and reflections' were 'industriously spread abroad, as is presumed to make me odious not only to the city but to all my friends.'

Francis Dickson, the printer, added to the speech the point that it was left to the public to think about how far they had been misled by 'sham speeches' put about in relation to Charles Donnell.

CHAPTER 4

Tory Gangs and Turncoats
1720s

*'But this I further for my innocency declare, I never
had intention to rob Mr. Kennersly… .'*
LAST SPEECH OF JAMES STEVENS

In those remarkable documents, the last dying
speeches of the condemned, we have several sources
of great insight into the nature of crime in times
past, and in eighteenth century Dublin in particular.
Thanks to the work of writer James Kelly, we have an accessible
collection to peruse and in that reading, we find the criminal
underworld of the Georgian period laid open to us.

These were speeches compiled often from the death cell. In
Newgate there was a tradition that the ordinary (or warder)
would put together these biographies from the mouths of the
people about to die. As we might expect, there were many
different varieties of these, but there are common areas of
writing: they usually have some kind of remorse and confession;
they recount the particulars of the offence; sometimes they are
in a moral and religious tone, and in many cases there is an
extended defence of what the crime has been, with suitable
words spoken to parents, moral guides, authority or even to the
poor families about to be bereft of a member of their clan.

But for understanding the range of crimes in the period, and
also in their revelations of how crime functioned, they are
valuable documents. The other feature is, of course, that they
are in the first person, and so they may seem at times as though
they are monologues from the very heart of a life on the edge, a
life about to face eternity.

In a cluster of speeches from one period, the 1720s and
1730s, we can gather some very typical criminal lives; the story
of James Stevens, for instance, hanged at Stephen's Green in
May 1726, for 'feloniously taking from Mr Philip Kennersly of
Dame Street, a glass case, value £50', we have a reminder of the

severity of the 'Bloody Code' of capital offences in Georgian Britain. Stevens protested his innocence (as almost every prisoner does) and gave as his reason for bothering to make a speech, that he wanted those who had lied about him to be revealed. He gave their names: 'Considerations move me to make this, my only and last, were I not sensible of the many villainous falsities which might be published …by persons of the vilest characters.. such as one Hoy in Pembroke-Court.'

Stevens was born in London and had been brought up to a trade, in portraiture. He was given an apprenticeship and did well. But wanting to see the world, he joined the army and travelled abroad. Returning home, he went into the licensed coaches business, and even had dealings with wealthy people such as the Blounts; but we do not know what the 'many

The 'Black Dog' Debtors' Prison. The author

misfortunes' were that came on him and made him leave for a new life in Ireland. But he came to Dublin and followed his trade, but then he met a woman who he argued was the cause of his ruin. He even named her: Eleanour Fenly. She also had a brother who participated in ruining him, a certain Fernando Fenly. Fernando it was who 'grassed' on Stevens: he said that 'about the 25th of March last I had a box of goods which were Mr. Kennerly's, afterwards found in his custody, and that I paid him two shillings for carriage from the Sun Inn in Francis Street...'

Stevens then seems to have become embroiled in fights and general street crime, mixing with Eleanour and a man called Byrne. He says that he acquired a bad reputation; but whatever the truth, his line of thought here is that he was, as we say today, 'fitted up' and sent for trial. The world he was moving about in was very much like that described by Daniel Defoe in his novel, *Moll Flanders* (1722) in which we have an insight into the class divisions in that society and also into the tremendous risks taken by those who looked for opportunities for shop-lifting and burglary. With over 200 capital crimes on the statute books, a thief was more than likely to either be hanged or transported merely for the theft of an animal or a yard of cloth.

But there was more to Stevens than the man we have through reading this speech. As we match his statement with those made by an accomplice, a small area of the criminal underworld is momentarily lit up for the modern reader. Although there is a lot of criminal

The College Buck, a print from 1754.

Author's collection

literature available for the Georgian underclass, much of it has been distorted by film and popular media. The truth under that is that the life at the bottom of society was 'nasty, brutish and short' and that we have to rely on reading between the lines to find something near the truth of many of these crimes and their strange narratives.

Whatever the truth of Stevens' words, the fate in store for him still opens up great pity in us. But one thing is certain – the Kennersly robbery was an affair that brought down another man – Patrick Barnel. Barnel was charged as an accomplice, and from his statement we learn more of the crime. There is only a hint of what might have been behind all this: Barnel was what was then called a 'Molly' or sodomite, at least, according to one writer. He said that he was involved in the robbery and that he 'gave up some of the things' in the hope of saving his life. That

Ormonde market today. The author

was to no avail, but the printer of the last dying speeches gave us a tantalising scrap of detail, as he was the writer who publicly called the man a sodomite. Barnel said: 'The printer hereof... unwittingly galled him ...saying he looked like death, when a person affirmed to his face, in the open street, he said he was a MOLLY... a charge so bold that it might be wished, before he strives to taint another's he clear his own character from that aspersion, so it may be termed...'

This gives us something of the human story behind the bare facts of the last speeches. Here were two men about to die together, and the first is concerned to name the alleged turncoats who gave him in, and the other wants to clear his name.

But Barnel had more to say, and his speech as printed by a printer in Castle Street, brings in the Tory Gangs. 'Tory' was the name given in the late seventeenth century to the people thrown out of their land by English settlers; such unfortunates had no choice but to become outlaws and to live in the hills and remote

The alternative to the scaffold. Author's collection

places. By 1720 it was being used for outlaws and rogues in gangs about the land, and Barnel was one such criminal. He says that he was born in Dublin and was a thief from his very early days, but then later joined a gang:

> *I was induced to commit great rogueries; I became acquainted with a gang of tories who kept their rendezvous in the county of Kerry with whom I committed such cruel and barbarous actions that we were all obliged to disperse and shift every one for himself....*

Coming to Dublin, he soon joined another gang and from smaller thefts he lifted his game to stealing from the property of the wealthy; we have to surmise that he met Stevens and probably the Byrn and Fenly lot, and that the two newcomers were set up to fall.

Both men show aspects of that timeless quality of criminals – no honour amongst thieves. They both pointed the finger at individuals, even from the scaffold, and in Barnel's case, in both his statements he had a vindictive few words to say about the printers. As always in such literature, the villains are concerned about their image and reputation. Barnel today would probably be writing true crime books or telling his tales to a journalist.

CHAPTER 5

A Case of Abduction
1730

'Sometimes it was the end of an unfortunate courtship, and the girl was dragged away by the man she had refused...'
W E H LECKY

In the time when the Old Bailey was the centre of attraction for everyone on both sides of the law, there were tradesmen about who were only too happy to cash in on the sensational and sad lives of villains – especially those whose lives had ended dangling on a rope at Tyburn. One such retailer was Richard Wam of the *Bible and Sun* at Warwick Lane, Amen Corner, London. Among his sick and bizarre items for sale there was a series of chapbooks with narratives on them, and one of these published in 1730 was this, as advertised:

> *The case of Mr. Dan. Kimberley, attorney at law, executed at Dublin, May 27, 1730, for assisting Bradock Mead to marry Bridget Rending, an heiress. Contained in his declaration and dying words, delivered to the Rev. Mr. Derry, at the place of execution, and recommended to Dean Percival, John Hacket, Esq', and two other gentlemen, to see it published. Price: three pence.*

Behind that smart piece of advertising there lies not only the complex tale of a learned

Memorial at the corner of Stephen's Green. The author

and educated man who fell into deep trouble, but also a story typical of its age and place – one more abduction in hundreds, a trade (and a crime) totally heartless and unscrupulous – and of course, a capital offence. Kimberley's last dying speech tract was headed: 'Daniel Kimberly, Gentleman'. Those words were unusual for a gallows tale, and his date with death was as meticulously recorded as the vents of his own story:

> *Executed at St Stephen's Green on Wednesday, May 27th, 1730 at 38 minutes past three o'clock in the afternoon.*

The famous historian of eighteenth century Ireland, W E H Lecky, in his account of the spate of abductions of heiresses in that time, explains how many people ascribed them to sectarian enmity, yet he finds little evidence of that. But there were certainly many varieties of abduction, and whatever their nature, they were brutal and cruel. At its worst, an abduction could be like this one, as described by Lecky:

> *On a Sunday in the June of 1756, the Rev. John Armstrong was celebrating divine service in the Protestant church in the town of Tipperary, Susannah Grove being among the congregation. In the midst of the service Henry Grady, accompanied by a body of men armed with blunderbusses, pistols, and other weapons, called out to the congregation that anyone who stirred would be shot, struck the clergyman on the arm with a hanger and... hastening to the pew where Susannah was sitting, dragged her out...*

But we are not dealing with this variety in Kimberly's story, and, as Lecky points out, the Kimberly case is unusual because he was a Protestant, pointing out that 'Among the few persons who were executed for abduction in Ireland was an attorney named Kimberly, at a time when no-one but a professing Protestant could be enrolled in that profession.'

Here then, we have a case of a lawyer and a Protestant being hanged for an offence for which few were hanged. What was so heinous about this particular abduction? Or did Kimberly have powerful enemies?

His own account of the events of the abduction of Bridget

Reading (not Rending, as the London printer had it) is expectedly, full of bad luck stories and of his being an innocent dupe. Making sense of Kimberly's own garbled and complicated account of what happened, there emerges a bare outline of a plausible story: he was a lawyer and so would have appeared to be hardly a 'heavy' when it came to applying some pressure on the intended abduction and forced marriage of your

Lately publifh'd, in the fame Size with the Hiftory of Executions, and very Proper to be bound up with this Year's SET,

THE Cafe of Mr. Dan. *Kimberley*, Attorney at Law, Executed at *Dublin*, May 27, 1730. for affifting *Bradock Mead* to marry *Bridget Reading*, an Heirefs. Contained in his Declaration and Dying Words, deliver'd to the Revd. Mr. *Derry*, at the Place of Execution, and recommended to Dean *Percival*, *John Hacket*, Efqr; and two other Gentlemen, to fee it publifh'd. Pr. 2 d.

II. A Collection of Remarkable Cafes for the Inftruction of both Sexes, in the Bufinefs of Love and Gallantry. Being a modeft and clear View of the three following Tryals, *viz.* 1. Of *Richard Lyddel*, Efq; for a criminal Converfation with the Lady *Abergavenny*. 2. Of *Knox Ward*, Efq; for a Promife of Marriage to Mifs *Sarah Holt*. 3. Of Col. *Francis Ch-rt-is*, for a Rape committed on the Body of *Anne Bond*, his Servant. Containing the Subftance of three Sixpenny Pamphlets (call'd Tryals) on thefe Subjects. Price 6 d.

III. A Second Collection of Remarkable Cafes, *viz.* in Love and Law, in Phyfic, Scandal, and Religion. Containing, 1. The Tryal of Mr. *J. Whaley*, for Breach of a Marriage-Promife to Mrs. *Eliz. Davis*, late of *Haverford-Weft*; with the Subftance of feveral Love-Letters that pafs'd betwixt them. 2. The Tryal of *Eliz. Chamberlain*, on an Action brought againft her by *Samuel Stockwell*, alias, *Sam the Potter*, an Independant Parfon, for faying he was a Rogue, a Drunkard, a Libertine, and a Singer of bawdy Songs; with the merry Defence of his fanctified Reputation. 3. The Qualifications neceffary to fet up a raw Independent Parfon. 4. The Defcription and Character of a Novice. 5. A pleafant New Song on a King and a Young Lady. 6. A furprizing Account of the (fuppofed) Murder of a Gentleman by Pills, Potions, and Chirurgical Operations, in a Letter from a Rev. Divine to his Widow, who was going to marry the fufpected Murtherer. Price 6 d.

IV. *Scotch* Gallantry Difplay'd: Or, The Life and Adventures of the unparallel'd Col. *Fr-nc-s Ch-r-t-s*, impartially related. With fome Remarks on other Writers on this Subject. Pr. 6 d.

Kimberly's case made profits for printers. A Newgate advert. Author's collection

Bridget Reading, for that is what lies at the heart of this story. Kimberly was contacted by an unscrupulous adventurer called Braddock Mead, with an assignment of visiting the nurse who had the guardianship of Bridget. Now, Kimberly argued that the old couple who had Bridget in care were also after her inheritance, and he said that he was told 'there was a considerable sum of money due to her... she never having received a penny from her father, who was an ill man'.

The lawyer then found out that Mead, back in London, had more knowledge of Bridget's situation than he had at first said because he took out articles with a man called Dodamy with a plan to sell Bridget's estate for the then huge sum of £3,600. The pressure was then on Kimberly to get a desired result in his negotiations to prise Bridget from her guardian and to speed her to the altar with Mead. Again and again, Kimberly insisted that there had been no forced marriage: 'soon after, and by my consent, and inducement, Mead applied to said Bridget by way of courtship and on 11th April, 1728, said Mead married her in Dublin, when and where no force, threats, or compulsion was made use of by any person towards said Bridget to come into said marriage.'

Understanding this case is all a matter of believing that Kimberly was 'sold out' to the law or not. His argument was that Mead was largely responsible for duping him and setting him up, as he was seen as the actual agent of the affair, and so would be assumed to have used force on the girl. When Mead was arrested and imprisoned and the network was about to be destroyed (and heads to roll) Mead was threatened by Mr Reading to apply a charge of rape against him unless he had the marriage annulled, Kimberly was apparently 'stooged.' He did understand that the right moves had been attempted, though. Applications were made to the Doctors' Commons, and though the intentions may have been good, to dissolve the contract, perhaps the Doctors' Commons was not the right place to go. Later, Dickens was to call that institution of Doctors of Law 'a cosy, dozy, old-fashioned and time-forgotten, sleepy-headed little family party'.

As with all such convoluted narratives of crime, it all depends who is believed at the time, and by the people who matter. Daniel Kimberly was clearly not believed; we have his side of the story, but we also have the weight of history and statistics to show how hard the authorities were coming down on abductions of heiresses. It may be that, in the end, Kimberly was being harshly punished as a precedent to other professional gentleman not be involved in that nefarious and amoral trade.

He faced his death on the scaffold with courage, offering some dramatic entertainment to the crowd. He even ended his speech with the surprising attitude of forgiveness: 'As for my prosecutors, or such as have persecuted me. Or fought any perjurious or indirect ways to take away my life, I freely forgive them.' Reading between the lines, there is still rancour there, and a 'spin' towards showing himself in a better light than his enemies. But, as with many others in his final minutes, his main concern was for his reputation:

In order to prevent the publishing of any false or spurious accounts of me... I do therefore humbly entreat my very worthy friends, the Rev. Dean Percival, Mr Derry, John Hacket, Edmund Fenner... to order the printing and publishing of this declaration.

He did have some friends (Dean Percival has gone down in history as one of the men who lampooned Jonathan Swift in a satirical poem) but clearly their exertions were not strenuous enough to save him from the gallows.

CHAPTER 6

Liberty and Ormond Boys
1730–1790

*'There they stripped him naked, then with a brush … they daubed
him over with warm tar, then a bag of feathers was got …'*
J D HERBERT

A liberty is an area of a borough outside the jurisdiction of the local authorities, and in Dublin these institutions go back a very long way into the Middle Ages when they were places outside the city walls. There were traditionally fifteen liberties, and for centuries the symbolic defending of the liberty boundaries was a grand affair. These areas were at one time in the possession of the Earl of Meath, and it was through him that the Huguenot weavers were brought into the area; these were Protestants persecuted in France, particularly after the revocation of the Edict of Nantes

Memorial in the Liberties. The author

'Guinness' houses in the Liberties today. The author

(which had previously given them protection) in 1685.

In John O'Keefe's memoirs he gives an account of this ceremony: 'The Lord Mayor walked the boundaries, his sword-bearer before him; but when he arrived at the point where the Liberty begins, he was met by a certain chosen number of people who stopped his progress and in a kind of seeming scuffle, took the sword from the sword-bearer.'

Dublin people in the eighteenth century must have prayed that such confrontation could have stayed ceremonial, because on the contrary, such was the clannish opposition between the weavers and the butchers that there was often gang warfare. The Huguenots were always involved in the textile trade, notably in silk manufacture and they had settled in large numbers; a gang from the weaving community known as the Liberty Boys from the Coombe, around St Patrick's cathedral, and their arch-enemies were the butcher boys from the Ormond market, and so known as the Ormond Boys.

The weavers had been aggressive in the face of a decline in trade as people bought foreign cloth, and quite often gangs of weaver boys would roam around victimising anyone seen wearing foreign clothes. J D Herbert, in his book *Irish Varieties*, gives an account of their reign of terror at its worst, and here he describes what the gangs did when they found a trader who had made or sold goods from these imported fabrics:

> *... they brought him perhaps to Liberty Square... There they stripped him naked; then with a brush, not camel's hair, they daubed him over with warm tar; then a bag of feathers was got, and everyone who could get at the victim stuck the feathers over him: then they led him in mock triumph through the Liberties, and when saturated, let him get home if he was able.*

This was surely terrifying, but was nothing to compare with what tended to happen when the Ormond and Liberty boys turned really nasty.

In a word, an encounter when they met was soon escalating into a riot. One of the most intense and violent periods for these clashes was in 1748, when there were fights every night in Aungier Street and sometimes in Phoenix Park. In that park on

The special criminal court, Green Street.   The author

one occasion the Liberty gang captured a butcher and a report of the time states that the victim was 'hacked in so terrible a manner that he is past giving any further disturbance to the public'. But as with all gang warfare, there was vengeance, and the Ormond gang did so by slamming a weaver on a meat-hook on St Audeon's Gate.

We can tell how extreme and zealous these gangs were when we look at the wildness and criminality these men took with them when they crossed the water to England as well. For instance, one Garret Lawler was a butcher's apprentice from Dublin and he broke his indentures and ran away to Liverpool and became a gambler and conman. One of the leaders of the Ormond and Liberty riots was a man called Thomas Quinn, a buckle-maker. He joined a London gang and was eventually involved in major crime and his destiny was the Tyburn gallows. The Dublin mob were fond of barbaric retribution – often

Mary Dagoe fights on the scaffold, from an old print. Author's collection

The Huguenot Cemetery. The author

mutilation and ham-stringing of victims. There were women in
these outfits as well, and some left Dublin for London, such as
Hannah Dagoe, who was described as 'a lusty, strong, bold-
spirited woman'. She had a capital offence against her and went
to the scaffold, but as the Newgate ordinary wrote, 'she was not
easily hanged, knocking the hangman out of the cart before a
company of sheriff's officers subdued her so the hangman
could do his work in earnest'.

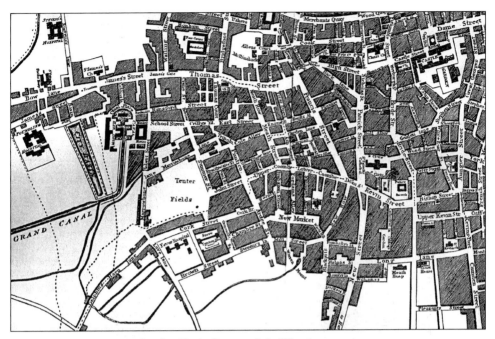

1829 map showing Kevin Street and the Liberties. Author's collection

In Dublin, arguably one of the very worst atrocities in the gang conflict was the attack on an infamous villain known as Paul 'Gallows' Farrell. In truth, he was so offensive that he had made enemies of both tribes, so they joined forces for revenge. Farrell was a city constable turned informer and at the time, ten at night on the 23 August 1734, he was being escorted to prison. He was taken and attacked about the head and even one of his testicles was cut off. He was ignominiously dragged through the streets to Chamber Street and there he was hanged. There he was left until the authorities cut him down the following day. The forces of law and order were often confronted by the gangs in this period: in 1729 there had been an attack on watchmen in Kevin Street, in daylight, with bold and brutal violence done against the officers of the law.

There was something even more threatening towards the end of that restless and anarchic century: the council of the city tailors became militarised to assert its rights and power, and a cadre known as the Liberty Light Horsemen was formed. In the year in which revolution hit France, Dublin also had a major

St Audoen's, with a new gate. The older one was where a victim's head was placed.

Author's collection

riot, instigated by these rogues. There was a terrible riot and people died, including a police constable. The Liberty Light Horse may be compared to the Australian bushrangers in a way, mobile and without morals, liable to strike anywhere, as two of them did in 1790 when they attacked a timber yard. They were caught and hanged by Newgate prison on Green Street. Not long after, the mastermind of that nefarious gang, Charles Wall, was caught and transported for an attack on a clothier.

St Audoen's today. The author

We can gauge just how violent the times were by noting some statistics: between 1780 and 1795, 232 men and ten women were hanged in Dublin, according to the *Hibernian Journal.* That means that there were around twelve a year, from a population of about 180,000. It appears, through English eyes, as an accelerated pattern compared to the English 'Bloody Code' in which, to put it simply, the propertied hanged the propertyless.

As the gangs linked to trades and occupations, they sank into the menacing and underhand existence of secret societies, oath-taking and in extreme cases, arson of the property of the opposition. There is no wonder that it was in Dublin, in 1786 that the Police Act was passed, making the first centralised police force in Britain and Ireland.

Near the end of this tumultuous century there were food riots in the Liberties, and once again, out came the gallows, busy both at Newgate and at Kilmainham common and in the gaol itself. It takes an effort of the imagination, walking the tourist-packed streets of Dublin today, to imagine the anarchy and barbarity abroad in the city in the 1780s and 1790s, but it was indeed one of the worst locations for sheer violent unease and fear in the whole of Europe. The gang warfare earlier in the century had laid the foundations for the kinds of escalation of disorder we find in the revolutionary period, the time when, after all, Dublin lawyer Wolfe Tone and his associates, was about to try to lead a rebellion against England in 1798. To make sense of all this street crime and physical threats from one faction to another, we can point to both political and economic distress and disquiet. But in the so-called 'Age of Reason' the pleasures of the Enlightenment were for the wealthy majority: for most it was make some solidarity or sink into a morass of poverty and deprivation.

CHAPTER 7

The Lord Santry Trial
1739

*'Santry himself notched the barrel of his pistol to mark
each deed of blood.'*
GEOFFREY ASHE

In eighteenth century Dublin the Hell-Fire club met at Daly's club on College Green, and other places rather more in keeping with the Hell-Fire traditions. These were basically organisations which were formed by the bored and rakish sons of the aristocracy, often in old ruins or halls on country estates; they were places where immorality of various kinds could be indulged and practised. They also had ritualistic tendencies, often involving sexual and drunken orgies.

In Dublin, the Hell-Fire club acquired the local name of 'The Devil's Kitchen' and the rascals associated with it were known as 'bucks'. The club was founded by Richard Parsons, Earl of Rosse and Colonel Jack St Leger. These characters were out for a good time and with no sense of restraint. Their motto was 'do as you will'. The wildness of their parties may be illustrated by

College Green, with the Bank of Ireland, 1878. The Graphic

the tale of Buck Sheely, a man who was caught cheating at cards; after a mock trial, the victim was thrown through the window on the third floor, and he was dressed up as a bull, with actual skin and horns used. It was no joke though, as Sheely died.

In the 1730s in Dublin, a leading group of these rogues was painted by James Worsdale, and his work is in the Irish National Gallery; it shows Lord Santry, Simon Luttrell (the Earl of Carhampton), the colonels Clements, Ponsonby and St George. When this picture was done, Santry was a young rake in his twenties and, as with so many of his peers, he had a penchant for a good, exciting duel. As historian Geoffrey Ashe has written, 'Santry himself notched the barrel of his pistol to mark each deed of blood.'

But Santry was to become an infamous figure in criminal history in 1739, because his mad antics went too far on one occasion, and he took a life – that of footman Laughlin Murphy. The official account of the trial, which took place at the Dublin House of Commons, contains a huge amount of pomp and circumstance; after all, the lords were trying one of their own. Santry was Henry Barry. He had succeeded to the title of the fourth Lord Santry in January 1735.

The occasion of the trial (27 April) was highly militaristic as well as being colourful and solemn as such major trials were at the time. There was a regiment of infantry on College Green and also a company of battle-axe guards along the road to Parliament House. Santry was twenty-nine, and he was taken very early to the court. Waiting for him were the panel of judges and the Lord High Steward. A manuscript written about the event describes the opening of the proceedings:

> *The proclamation was made, that the person or persons to whom any writ or precept had been directed, for the certifying any indictment or record before The Lord High Steward, should certify and bring in the same forthwith... Whereupon the writ of certiori, with the precept to the Lord Chief Justice.. were delivered in at the table and read by the Clerk of the Crown of the King's bench, whereupon the sheriffs of the city of Dublin gave in the writ for bringing up the prisoner...*

The Four Courts, seat of justice. The author

This has all the tenor and import of something heavily serious, indicating that there was something momentous about the fact that a rake and a Hell-Fire member had been brought to justice. Santry was then brought to the bar; he made three reverences and a salute was returned. Clearly, here was no ordinary trial of a petty criminal.

The crime had allegedly been committed in a public house in Palmerstown on 9 August in the previous year. Santry and his bucks were in a room in the tavern enjoying themselves and Murphy was in the kitchen, linked to the room by a narrow corridor. Murphy was employed as a general servant really, doing such things as carrying messages, being a porter and helping in travel arrangements. He was a married man with three children and the Attorney General at the trial made a point of saying that poor Murphy was 'a person who with a good deal of industry and difficulty maintained himself and family...'

After the main celebrations of the evening had passed and most guests had left, an argument developed between Santry and a man called Humphreys. Everyone was intoxicated, as witnesses stated. One witness, Jocelyn, testified that Santry had twice tried to draw his sword to set about attacking Humphreys that night.

Santry raged out down the passage to the kitchen and there he bumped into Murphy. He shoved him away and shouted that he would kill the next man who said a word. For some reason, Murphy did speak, and they were his last words. The drunken Santry, totally out of control, stabbed his servant and mortally wounded him. But he was a long time dying. On the night of the stabbing, so the writer of the trial report said:

> The poor man spoke, and the noble Lord the prisoner too punctually performed what he had so rashly sworn and stabbed him. Upon this the man went into a room near the kitchen, stayed but a little while, and came back into the kitchen; the blood gushed out of the wound, the man fell down and cried out, I am killed...

As for Santry, drunk as he was, he mounted his horse and thought he could buy silence by giving £4 to the landlord. He gave no directions as to what should be done or whether help might be called.

Laughlin Murphy took a long time to die: he passed away on 25 September, in Hammond Lane in the city. That fact was the saving of Santry. Because death had not been instant, there was an opening for the defence counsel of course – that it had been disease that had actually caused the death. There was no high-lighting of such factors as the fact that no medical help had been called, no remorse expressed, and so on. The buck had merely thrown a coin and implied that it had better be all hushed up.

Where the turning point lay which led to the acquittal through a reprieve from the King is up for discussion, but certainly a letter written by Dr Thomas Rundle, Archbishop of Perry, mentions one important figure – the Solicitor General, Bowes. Rundle wrote that 'He did not use one severe word against the unhappy Lord, nor omitted one severe observation that truth could dictate.. But I think the Counsel for the prisoner acted detestably. They only prompted him to ask a few treacherous questions…'

In other words, justice was done, because there had quite clearly been the most terrible and callous behaviour on the part of this notorious buck and scoundrel. As Rundle wrote, still with a bitterness in his tone:

> *When the 23 peers returned to give their opinion, their coun-tenances astonished the whole house, and all knew, from the horror in their eyes, and the paleness of their looks, how they were agitated within before they answered the dread question 'Guilty upon my honour' and he was so most certainly, according to the law…*

But Santry never went to the scaffold. In fact, he was awarded a full pardon. The Duke of Devonshire, the Lord Lieutenant of Ireland, had been largely responsible for petitioning George II. If Santry had gone to meet his death, it would have been a beheading; but he lived to carry on his rakish life. He was also attainted, meaning that he had to forfeit his estate, but that was returned to him after the pardon in 1740. A year after his pardon, Santry travelled to see King George II and thanked him face to face; his pardon had come from the Lords Triers who had found him guilty, but all except one of them signed a letter asking for a pardon. As soon as he had seen the king in Germany, the process of redeeming his estates started.

On his death, the Santry title became extinct.

CHAPTER 8

Fatal Duels
1750–1820

*'The cause of the quarrel was some joke which a Mr O'Hara
had made at the expense of Mr Napoleon Finn...'*

I n 1777, the practice of duelling was so rife that Ireland had to sort out some kind of regulations. The men involved came up with an Irish Code and this was always referred to as the 'Twenty-six Commandments'. The interesting point about that event is that the men who decided on the commandments were at Clonmel Assizes at the time. Maybe they had done the legal business and had time to spare, so they put together some rules for what had always been a chaotic affair, with insults being given and responded to in all areas of the land where the gentry and their profligate sons were active.

The problem with the duel has always been that there was no scale of insults which was generally agreed on. As the historian V G Kiernan has explained: 'For some offences an exchange of two or more shots was held to be the minimum purgation. Cheating at cards was one of the crimes equivalent to a blow. An enlightened provision was that challenges should not be delivered at night 'for it is desirable to avoid all hot-headed proceedings'. Irish heads were usually 'too well heated at night with claret'.

Frontispiece for Bosquett's A Treatise on Duelling, *1818.* Author's collection

A TREATISE

ON DUELLING;

TOGETHER WITH THE

Annals of Chivalry,

THE

ORDEAL TRIAL, AND JUDICIAL COMBAT,

FROM THE EARLIEST TIMES.

By ABRAHAM BOSQUETT, Esq.

Qui ante non cavet, post dolebit..
Ay me! what perils do environ
The man that meddles with cold iron;
HUDIBRAS.

LONDON

1818.

From the beginnings of recorded history in Ireland there had been duels, even extending back to folklore and myth. But when the Restoration brought with it a conquest of the land by the Anglo-Irish class, duelling became a part of the ideology of their power and indeed their culture. A duel became a very common matter. The Victorian historian Froude referred to these people as 'Irish chiefs of the sixteenth century in modern costume.' Being engaged in duelling was a crucially important part of the code of being a 'gentleman' of course and it was often said that a man was not able to take his place in the hierarchy of that power of the landed gentry until he had 'smelt powder'.

In the eighteenth and early nineteenth centuries, there are numerous duels. Some of them involved famous characters and others concerned obscure people. Even Wolfe Tone acted as a second in a duel while at Trinity College, and one of his friends died in that encounter. So common was the habit that even the provost of the college was a duellist at one point. One particular area around the city was known for its duels – a place known as Clontarf Wood. The reputation of that place was that it was 'where men of heart go to bleed one another in duels'.

One of the very last duels in Dublin took place in 1838, when a Galway man called O'Hara made a joke at the expense of Robert Napoleon Finn. He refused to apologise and the duel had to go ahead, so seconds were appointed and the assignation was settled, to take place at North Bull, around three miles from Dublin. They arrived at the scene and put their coats on the

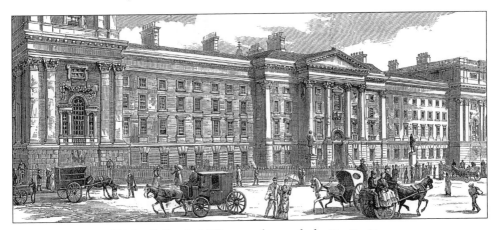

Trinity College in 1878, scene of many duels. The Graphic

sand; a man called Ireland was a witness and he later gave an account of what happened to William Le Fanu.

An experienced second said he would give the signal to fire and the two men stood at each side of him, ready to walk their twelve paces. What happened next was farcical. The second said that there would just be the one signal, the words, 'Ready, fire'. But the nervous Finn, when he heard the man say the word fire, turned and pointed the pistol at him. The second told him to settle down, saying, 'Do you want to shoot me?' What followed was more like something from a melodrama:

> *At the word 'fire' Finn again lost his head, pulled the trigger of his pistol, which was pointed downwards, and lodged the bullet in the calf of his own leg. O'Hara, thinking that Finn had shot at him, immediately took aim at him, crying out, 'For God's sake, don't fire. It was all a mistake!' But O'Hara did fire, and his bullet struck the ground close to Finn.*

W R Le Fanu, 1893. Author's collection

Memoirs of a famous duel – Le Fanu's book, 1893. Author's collection

SEVENTY YEARS OF IRISH LIFE

BEING

ANECDOTES AND REMINISCENCES.

BY

W. R. LE FANU.

SECOND EDITION.

LONDON:
EDWARD ARNOLD,
37, BEDFORD STREET, STRAND, W.C.
Publisher to the India Office.
1893.
(All rights reserved.)

Mr Ireland, watching from close by, was sprayed with sand and then, before any more developments could take place, four constables arrived and arrested everyone who was present. They were all put into carriages and taken back to Dublin. Ireland points out that Finn's injured leg was dangling out of a carriage to keep it cool. A Dublin joker said that Finn had gone to the Bull, got cow'd and shot the calf.

The famous Daniel O'Connell was also involved in a Dublin duel. After he criticised the Dublin corporation, he made enemies, and a character called D'Esterre challenged him to fight. O'Connell was a married man, having wed Mary, his cousin, in 1802. There was no doubt that D'Esterre had provoked the argument, but it went to the actual confrontation and he was shot. It took him a few days to die, but before he did so he exonerated O'Connell from any blame, and his second, Sir Edward Stanley, made it clear to O'Connell that there would be no prosecution. O'Connell was later to be on the wrong side of the law (while he was Mayor of Dublin) and was in jail for three months for conspiracy.

Aubrey de Vere, in his memoirs, says that 'In those days (1830s) a duel was the most mirthful of pastimes' and he described a meeting of two lawyers in Dublin who met at sunrise in Phoenix Park; 'one was the biggest and one the smallest' in Dublin society. But the big man had problems with his eyesight and said he could not see his opponent. The other instructed his second to draw a white chalk line of his own shape on the large 'carcass' of his opponent. Such jocularity in chatty memoirs does not even hint at the terrible tragedies that occurred in duels, such as the fight in 1786 between Robert Keon of Leitrim and George Nugent Reynolds. Keon and

Reynolds arrived at the place for the duel before their seconds and went on without them; Keon shot Reynolds dead, then he was tried, found guilty and hanged, in March 1788.

In the late eighteenth century there had been some really prominent duels and some, such as a fight between Blaquerre and Bagenal in 1773, had such an effect that there was a public condemnation of the whole nasty business. But for a long time it was impossible to outlaw the practice; all that happened over the course of these years was that the fights were regulated, but not banned. There was always the added problem that when it was linked to army life and manners, there was a code of honour which ran contrary to the law.

Some duels were so high profile that they affected public opinion, and one notable confrontation between Flood and Agar led to duelling being given more general respect and support. This was because Flood, being accused of bribing

Liberator O'Connell in O'Connell Street. The author

magistrates, had such support and sympathy from the new middle classes that they took an interest in the case and in the words of one historian, the duel was 'the talk of the salons as well as the coffee houses'. The outcome was that duelling and its supporting code of honour, were understood and perhaps tolerated more by the public.

It has often been said and written that the notion of a duel, which is of course linked inextricably to notions of honour, reputation and class status, is deeply set in the Irish folklore and literature of earlier times. So much was this embedded in the later stereotypes of Irish character that the 'stage Irishman' of the eighteenth century English drama included the satirical depiction of the duelling temperament. The character of Sir Lucius O'Trigger in Sheridan's play *The Rivals* is typical of this. His name suggests his aggressive and volatile nature. That tradition of taking stock characters from Irish life and culture led to distortions and misunderstandings, but nevertheless, the historical record shows that Dublin people in these years had a penchant for settling disputes and matters of 'good name' by arranging a duel. The procedure and etiquette involved appealed so much to the general love of display and theatre that in terms of the media and the general civic gossip, at times a duel took its place as just another variety of slightly questionable but respected manly behaviour.

If we are to look for the kind of duel that would be more ordinary and typical, it would be the meeting between Standish O'Grady and Captain Smith in 1830. O'Grady, son of Edward O'Grady, chairman of the county of Waterford, was riding in Dawson Street when he smashed into a cabriolet driven by Captain Smith of the 32nd Regiment. O'Grady hit the officer's horse in order to free himself from the entanglement and Smith rounded on O'Grady and cracked him repeatedly with his own stick. O'Grady was merely a commissioner of bankrupts: Smith was a soldier, so the confrontation would be dangerous for the civilian generally, but he chased the cab and asked who had insulted him. Smith shouted out his name.

A message was sent by Lieutenant McNamara and they met at six in the morning, when O'Grady was shot, mortally wounded in the groin. Medical attention was given after he had been rushed to Richmond barracks, but he soon died.

CHAPTER 9

Trouble for the New Police
1780s

'The police will be a banditti in whom the people have no faith.'
HENRY GRATTAN

In Fishamble Street in 1778 five soldiers raped a woman in broad daylight. Some of them kept guard and pushed back any civilians who tried to intervene. In 1784, a drunken officer sexually assaulted the wife of a publican. These incidents illustrate the uneasy and sometimes savage relations between the Dublin populace and the militia. The usual consequences of an atrocity by the military was a reign of terror in which there were reprisals against the army, taking the form of tarring and feathering, and also that Irish speciality called 'houghing' – cutting of the tendons in the leg.

But even more influential on the radical actions taken to have proper law and order in the city was the general political situation. Politics is about strategies of power, and in the eighteenth century, from all kinds of roots in earlier English presence and plantation, what had been firmly established was government rule in Ireland from Westminster. In the years between 1586 and 1692 the Irish Parliament sat only fifteen times. The Irish House of Commons was controlled by England, with a system of patronage and pocket boroughs; in other words, there was no room for Irish people to have a fair representation (as in England also of course) but what made things worse in Ireland was the fact that three-quarters of the population, the Catholic people, were excluded from suffrage and from many other basic human rights, to say nothing of commercial and professional exclusions.

By the last few decades of the century though, not only had the American colonies won their independence from England by military force, but events in France, leading to the revolutionary events of 1789, were to have profound effects on

Ireland. By the 1719 Declaratory Act, the English parliament had put on the statutes the right to legislate for Ireland.

In the early 1780s, things began to change. In 1780 Henry Grattan tried to have a vote on Irish independence; it failed, but such failures only strengthened a desire to succeed and the Volunteer Movement took hold. This was a Protestant-based militia ostensibly to defend Ireland against the brewing attacks from the nationalists and their alliances with the French. But naturally, these men became a powerful force and when Grattan and other leaders made it clear that some kind of independence was desirable, they were seen by England as a potent threat to law and order.

The Volunteers had been founded in Belfast in 1778, but what was always threatening was the fact that they were not loyal to the crown. By 1779 they numbered over 100,000 men, and their leader was Lord Charlemont. An important detail in this context was that the Volunteers were allowed to carry arms; although there were severe penal laws used to suppress Ireland, these men were exempt because they were Protestant. It has been noted that they had a real presence, with their slogan, 'Free trade or a speedy revolution'.

Grattan did not want total independence; his vision was of the two parliaments linked in the enterprises of empire and commerce, but governed independently; in other words he wanted a partnership. After all, Irish men were a major supply of 'cannon fodder' for the imperial infantry and the general investment of riches and manpower in England from Ireland was on a large scale indeed.

By 1782, a number of changes in the law were effected and these have become known as the Constitution of 1782 and made it possible for the Lord Lieutenant of

Henry Grattan, from an old print. Author's collection

Ireland to have a major control of the legislature in the Irish House of Commons. It was all down to Grattan and the short-lived phase of Irish political history is known as Grattan's parliament.

For these political reasons, and for the general challenge to law in the city, by the 1780s it was plain to any observer that Dublin had a serious problem in terms of keeping the peace and protecting its citizens. The Irish Chief Secretary, Thomas Orde, who had been in disgrace with Pitt in England, was working to achieve something of importance and he saw that 'some regular and decisive amendment must be made in the police, for it is impossible yet to foresee, that a new mob may not in an instant renew the disturbances'. Earlier that year, the House of Commons itself had been under attack.

Before Orde brought in his new Police Act, Dublin's streets were ostensibly regulated by night watchmen, known as 'charlies', and they would carry a lantern and a pike, being merely a presence, rather than an active force against criminality. When Orde worked for his new act, he had to choose a model of policing and he had three options. First, he had London to look at, and policing there was hardly an inspiring matter. London had simply the Bow Street magistrates and the thief takers which had been set up by novelist and magistrate Henry Fielding and his brother John. Although reformers had put plans for new police before parliament, London was stagnant in that sense. Second, Edinburgh had its one hundred private soldiers, the town guard. These were certainly efficient. But it was France that eventually had the template Orde wanted.

The problem was that France was looked upon as a police state of course. The police force was an arm of the Ancien Regime – a terrible force for oppression with the use of spies and informers. But the man behind its adoption in Dublin was one Sackville Hamilton, clearly a more forceful decisive and forthright character than Orde. He made it happen. One of Hamilton's peers said of him, 'Without Hamilton I think no man in his senses would remain in Ireland for an hour.' He wrote a memorandum about the Paris police, using as a source the impressive volume, *The Police of France* (1763), by William Mildmay.

The watchmen had been so inefficient that people were making their own anti-crime initiatives, such as the formation of the Blackrock Felons' Association, led by William Ogilvie. He and his group aimed to take their own action against all the local villains in that Dublin suburb. Fortunately, there were wealthy people in Blackrock who could help to pay for such measures. Others were not so well placed.

The 1786 bill proposed to abolish the watchmen and to put a ward system into Dublin, run by a metropolitan police district. Three commissioners would control this, with a High Constable in total control. City magistrates were to be the men who took these new posts. There were several reasons why the new police were hated by some and welcomed by others: on the credit side, they would apply a measure of control over the too powerful army population. But on the debit side, the general population of Dubliners hated the idea. Grattan said that the police bill was 'the most obnoxious and alarming that ever, perhaps, arrested the attention of the Irish senate'.

The new police were seen by many as 'banditti' and many expected a reign of terror enforced by law. But of course there was plenty of street crime to fight, and some must have thought that at least they might be a little safer when they walked around

View of the Four Courts on the Liffey. The author

their own city. Writer J E Walsh, in 1847 describes one of the main threats – the 'Dublin footpads' of the 1780s:

The footpads congregated in a dark entry, on the shady side of the street if the moon shone; if not, the dim and dismal light of the lamps was little obstruction. A cord was provided with a

An alley off Grafton Street. The author

loop on the end of it. The loop was laid on the pavement, and the thieves watched the approaching pedestrian. If he put his foot in the loop, it was immediately chucked. The man fell prostrate and was dragged rapidly up an entry to some yard or cellar....Where he was robbed and sometimes murdered.

Yet naturally, for many people, the new police presence was deeply resented. There were attacks and assaults on officers in the early years, and the press was full of paranoid fears and talk of police spies in every public house and market place. Merely the sight of the new police, in uniform and on patrol, was proof that an alien concept had become a reality in the city streets. Perhaps things would have been different if Dublin had experienced public riot on a massive scale, as had happened a few years before, with the anti-Catholic Gordon Riots of 1780. But the inescapable fact was that many saw the whole development as an intolerable infringement of personal liberties.

It seems as though many had forgotten the state of affairs when all the good people of Dublin had between themselves and heartless criminals was the parish watch. The level of fear at the time was expressed by a letter written then and reprinted in 1988:

The higher sort were attacked in their carriages, plundered and abused, and put in fear and danger of their lives. The trader, after the close of day, was afraid to stir out of his house... the journeymen in dread carried his work home... old men, young women, servants and children were alike the prey of these rapacious villains.

CHAPTER 10

Sheriff Vance on Trial
1789

'His interference produced a riot; oyster shells and pebbles were thrown by the mob; the soldiers retaliated by firing on the people...'
A H ROWAN

The bloody sport of bull-baiting goes back many centuries, and opinions of it in society have been mixed. The whole business was done with that mix of ritual and carnival that characterised working class culture in past centuries; one account describes what tended to happen in this way: 'After a coming bull-baiting was advertised, the bull, decorated with flowers or coloured ribbons, would be paraded around the streets of the town... The parade ended, the bull, with a rope tied round the root of his horns, would be fastened to a stake with an iron ring in it, situated in the centre of a ring.'

What happened next was that the various dogs which had been made ready for an attack stood ready to be unleashed; there would follow a series of savage encounters in which lumps of flesh would be torn off the bull and there was a high chance that some dogs would die.

In England, a bill went to the Commons in 1802 to stop the barbarous practice, but was defeated. Not until 1835 did anyone succeed in abolishing it. But back in the eighteenth century it was a common pastime, and one event in 1789 in Dublin escalated into a bloody confrontation between the various people involved. This was just after Christmas that year and the scene turned into a bloodbath.

On St Stephen's Day, the working classes took their leisure and they were out to hold a bull-baiting session. They took a bull into a field enclosed by a high stone wall and preparations were being made for the entertainment, but there were people around who considered such things far from any kind of acceptable leisure pursuit and they sent for the authorities. The man who came to stop the baiting was Sheriff Vance and he sensibly brought troops with him. But the problem was that the crowd were not prepared to stand and watch as he stopped the proceedings. There was a riot.

Oyster shells and pebbles were thrown at Vance but in reply the soldiers retaliated by firing on the townsfolk. When a man called Ferral Reddy was shot dead, Vance found himself in trouble: in fact the Sheriff was arraigned for murder, and that was after friends of the dead man broadcast the situation, trying to turn public opinion against the man whose actions had led to an ordinary citizen being shot dead.

Archibald Hamilton Rowan was called to a meeting about the situation. Rowan was destined to be in trouble with the law himself just three years after these events; he had come to Ireland as a secretary to Sir Charles Montague and then, just a few years before this, joined the United Irishmen. When secretary of that organisation, he was arrested for seditious libel while in Black Lane in Dublin, and was given two years in Kilmainham, where the famous Wolfe Tone visited him. But in 1789 while he was living in Rathcoffey, he was called to help in the Vance affair.

Not only did Rowan, who loved notoriety and to be given the chance to attract attention, accepted the role of investigator and after that subscriptions were called for to finance the prosecution. With cash being raised and public sympathy with him, Rowan had a cause and he made sure that his actions were visible. As he wrote to his wife about what he had been doing:

> *I got down at Ellis's about twelve, and from that time until five I was tracing every step of the military on the fatal day; and the more inquiry I make, the more I am confirmed in the opinion of its being a most diabolical exercise of power. I saw the father and mother of one of the sufferers, whose story is itself a tragedy.*

There had been a grievous overreaction, for sure. Even in an era when savage repression of mobs and riots was often condoned, this was savage. Strictly, Vance should have followed the proper course of law and waited until he could find support and authority, then act with caution and discretion.

Dublin Castle entrance. The author

The nasty business was then studied and investigated by the court of the King's Bench, with Richard Power leading, and something very odd and paradoxical happened: in a long speech the Solicitor General discussed and analysed bull-baiting and concluded that it was 'both lawful and innocent' – so despite the fact that three men had been killed when Vance ordered his men to fire (the three were killed in Abbey Street) the fact that the soldiers had been surrounded and attacked led the lawyers to concentrate on that action, not the baiting, and so look with sympathy on Vance's actions that day.

The jury found Vance not guilty. Rowan pointed out how the law had let down the natural sense of justice: 'The law permits you not to kill him that assails you when you draw near your last refuge, because you foresee that you shall be driven to it, but you must forebear till that necessity be at the full period...' But Rowan saw the issues involved and understood the result: '... he thought that Vance had no justifiable necessity to plead, but he has been acquitted by his country... bold would be that man who dared to call him guilty.'

Many years before this, in 1715, the Riot Act had been established, laying down right and proper procedure to cope with a riot. A riot was defined as 'an unlawful assembly which has begun to execute its common purpose by a breach of the peace and to the terror of the public.' Such words as 'terror' and the execution of a 'common purpose' may well have applied to the bull-baiting situation, but they did things differently in the year of the French Revolution. The 1715 Act did also set down draconian punishments for those involved –even those who merely threw shells and pebbles – because an unlawful assembly was defined as a misdemeanour 'punishable by fines and imprisonment with hard labour'.

What Vance should have done was read a proclamation (he was a sheriff and so was entitled and qualified to do so) and in that he could have told the mob that anyone arrested could be given transportation for life. But ordering his men to fire was something done in sheer panic. Who knows just how threatening and intimidating the mob was? Through modern eyes his actions are insufferable and totally wrong, but 'Other times. Other moralities' seems to apply, and such things had a massive impact on legal judgements at a time when authoritarian power was the main focus of the criminal law and its sustenance in moments of anarchy and civil disorder.

But bull-baiting was far more serious than the mere act of a man refusing to drink to a toast of 'Confusion to the Country party', as James Eyre Weeks did in 1754; the mob that took upon itself to punish him could lead to a lynching. Weeks was offered a hundred guineas to repent but did not, and he was strung up. We might ask, where were the forces of law and order on that day? The victim was the publisher of *The Dublin Spy* and he was faced by a drunken mob of people against patriots. If a toast could lead to mob rule, then any gathering for loud entertainment could very easily do so, and most possibly, Vance was frightened for his life. The Riot Act was a luxury few people under severe pressure could afford to consider. The general feeling was that first you reach for your guns and then you ask questions.

CHAPTER 11

Delahunt, Child Killer
1841

*'While he was in that position, with his head drawn back,
I cut his throat.'*
JOHN DELAHUNT

There are some deviant types who linger on the edge of the law, filled with a mix of fascination and twisted egoism, like the characters who enjoy being present at a murder scene or who move around on the margins of police work and lawyers. Such a one was John Delahunt, a young man who liked to think he was valuable to the forces of law in 1840s Dublin. But he crossed the line into criminality, and in a sense he always was a lawbreaker. His story begins as a creepy and seedy life of a police informer and ends on the gallows.

In 1840 there had been a murder in Dublin – of an Italian boy, Garlibardo, and it had remained unsolved. Like its famous counterpart in London ten years before, it was a sensation. People spoke of a second 'Italian Boy' mystery killing, as they had done all over England. But in spite of the following tale of a child murder, there was to be no closure on that case.

In July 1841, a gang of roughs who were supporting O'Connell began harassing and shouting at Captain Craddock, a retired army man. The gang came to attack him when he was ill in bed, but such was the uproar and the level of fear that he was forced to raise himself into action. He grabbed a sabre and stood ready for them. The men, led by some malevolent types called Byrne and Courtney, at first threw bricks and wood at his door and windows, but then they smashed a door panel and forced their way in; one man hurled a brick at Craddock's chest and caused a severe wound. He then collapsed and was later taken to St Stephen's hospital.

The report at the time notes that at the trial, when of course the gang were identified, there was a note that 'The next witness called was a young man named Delahunt, who represented himself as being present at the outrage but asserted that he did not participate in it.' This is the first we hear of the murderous Delahunt. He was there as an informer. But we also learn something of his difficult and sick temperament, for he 'broke down' on that occasion, merely there as a witness.

Then, on Christmas Eve that year, a report was in *The Times* headed: 'Mysterious Murder: Coroner's Inquest.' The body of a young boy had been found murdered in a stable off Pembroke Road, near Baggott Street. The dead boy was around ten years old and apparently very poor; he had been battered on the head and his throat had been cut. Who was the man who reported the crime? It was John Delahunt, and the journalist had a good memory, noting that Delahunt had been 'one of the witnesses against Cooney, the tinker who was tried and acquitted of the murder of the Italian boy [July 1840]'. As we have seen in recent

Baggott Street, near where the body was found. The author

times with such killers at Ian Huntley, Delahunt was at the scene and was the first suspect. He was arrested and questioned.

The questioning immediately brought out some strange facts, mainly that he said he had seen a woman attacking the boy and that although he knew she was taking the child's life, he did not intervene. His statements were most suspect and made no sense. What sealed his fate was that two young girls, on separate occasions, said they had seen him with the boy. He had been seen at six in the evening in Upper Baggott Street leading a little boy along. She wasn't sure about the boy being the dead one, but then she was shown a hat belonging to the victim and she identified that as being worn by the boy walking with Delahunt.

Then Delahunt's brother and sister also gave statements to the effect that they also had seen him walking with the boy; Thomas his brother, said he had met them and asked the boy's

Parliament Hill, a favourite haunt of the killer. The author

name: it was Thomas Maguire. The coroner was satisfied that John Delahunt had been guilty of wilful murder and he was committed to Kilmainham Gaol. As for Delahunt, he 'betrayed no surprise and was in no degree discomposed'.

On 29 December, a report about Delahunt linked him to the murder of the Italian boy a year earlier, and the writer noted that he had been 'a sort of spy-informer by the police authorities'. When Cooney had been tried for that killing, Delahunt had been a prominent witness, after being on the fringes of Cooney's life, waiting and watching. The reporter was pleased to announce that 'he has been dismissed from the disreputable employment, which if such espionage could safely be dispensed with, he ought never to have held'.

He had been walking around Dublin Castle, wherever he could, in the hope of finding more work with the police; he stated that he was longing for what he called 'a situation'.

That report tells a great deal about the life of young Maguire and his mother. This was important, as Delahunt was trying to pin the murder on Mrs Maguire, saying he saw her there that night. He knew her clothes and described, in his lie, what she had been wearing, so that would have seemed a sound statement. The boy's mother had been deserted by her husband and had struggled to survive, opening a cake shop with her meagre savings, and with help from neighbours, she had managed to scrape together an existence. Her husband had returned from England to Dublin but had had nothing to do with his wife and son.

On the morning of the day on which the murder took place, Mrs Maguire was taken to Coombe Lying-in Hospital. It had been discovered by the reporters that she had been wearing the clothes described by Delahunt that day, as she went to hospital. This suggests the kind of devious and insidious infiltration of a family by a man with psychopathic tendencies; he had ingratiated himself into their confidence, using his close knowledge to create not only an alibi, but a fabricated narrative of a murder that never took place except in his mind. Mrs Maguire was so ill she knew nothing of what had happened.

The Maguires lived at Cherry Lane, near Great Britain Street, and young James worked as a market boy. Early on the fatal day, Delahunt had also been seen with Maguire in the

Drake's public house in Capel Street. The killer had been around the place when other boys had been playing with James, and they remembered Delahunt. He had been well known as someone who loitered about the area and was apparently friendly and approachable. The witnesses who were older had identified the body when it was first taken to Irishtown police station.

Not long after the coroner's court, Mrs Maguire was told of the events; she had been so desperately ill that the facts had been kept from her, and a report on the impact of that knowledge was that 'the shock was so overwhelming that the wretched woman sank under it and that no hopes are held of her ultimate recovery'. Another report said that she had died that day.

There was also talk of the unsolved murder of Garlibardo, the Italian boy killed the year before, and writers and reporters were saying that Delahunt was a likely suspect for that. There had been some nosing around and one investigator found that

On Capel Street, Delahunt liked the pubs and coffee-houses. From an 1890
directory. Author's collection

'Delahunt was cognizant of the frightful deed' and that he may even have killed a 'huxter' called Doolan near Drogheda, as it had been ascertained that Delahunt was living in that area when the murder happened.

Delahunt was tried and found guilty. He was to hang at Kilmainham and it was not long before he was visited by his father who had urged him to make a full confession. The Times reporter pointed out that 'The meeting is said to have been most heartrending… Delahunt is at present lying in the hospital attached to the gaol, with strength so prostrated that many think he will not survive till the day intended for his execution.'

His confession stated that the evidence against Cooney for the Italian Boy murder had been false but denied any guilt for that himself. Just days before the execution, the Governor of the prison, Mr Alison, spoke with Delahunt and they discussed the Italian Boy case; Alison had apparently gone to see him not to order but to implore him to come clean on anything he knew about that unsolved case, impressing upon him the importance of that information for all kinds of reasons. Delahunt agreed that he would write something.

Delahunt did indeed write that he knew nothing and was not involved, and in his last hours, a reporter was allowed in to see him. What followed was entirely typical of those times, when many people believed that the 'science' of phrenology' could tell criminal types by the bumps on their heads. The report for the hospital where the murderer lay was:

> He was seated at a table before a fire; his head rested on one side on his right hand, but in such a manner… that his face was completely concealed from view. He held his prayer book, to which he appeared to devote his closest attention.. and seemed perfectly indifferent to the presence of any other person… A phrenological survey of his head had led others to the sapient conclusion that because the 'bump of destructive-ness' is rather strongly developed, the murderer could not be held accountable for his own actions.

In his statement, the events of that murderous act were known fully for the first time. He wrote that he had done so many iniquitous things, it was a case of utter amoral, brutal hunger for

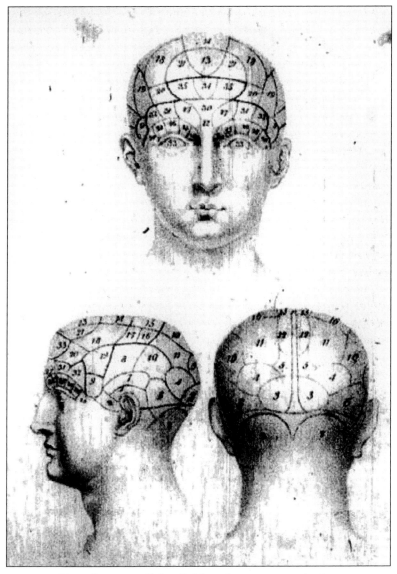

Phrenology, as applied to Delahunt by an expert at the time,
from the Ladies Magazine, 1833. Author's collection

money and for attention. He even said he had lied when he informed against some of the men accused of the attack on Craddock. But when it came to the murder of young Maguire, the account of the killing makes hard reading:

He raised up his head to make me feel more easily. His back was then to me, and at that moment, with his head drawn back, I cut his throat and threw him from me. He fell on his face. He uttered no cry, nor did he make any noise whatever. On getting about three yards from him I looked back and saw him on his feet again. I did not clean the knife, but threw it into the field.

He said that he could not explain why he killed the boy, but admitted that he had been planning the killing for two months.

Delahunt was hanged on 6 February 1842, after waking up and drinking some tea and saying some last prayers. A massive police presence was gathered outside the walls, and after a breakfast at nine o'clock, the killer was led out to the scaffold. Other prisoners on his route to the last stand in life knelt and prayed as he passed. Delahunt had already had his arms pinioned in the chapel before the walk to the noose; when he was placed on the drop, his resolve failed and he collapsed. So the bolt was slid and he was executed. One witness said that his end was speedy, taking three minutes to die on the end of the rope. That is not fast by the standards of the Pierrepoints in the twentieth century of course, but in the 1840s, it was quite a professional job.

No-one present shouted or said anything offensive. The crowd of 20,000 people stood around until the man was cut down and his body taken into the gaol cemetery. It was after that when the confession was publicised. The world was reassured by the opening words of that paper, written down by Father Patrick Reilly: 'I state positively that I had neither hand, act nor part in the death of Garlibardo, the Italian boy…'.

CHAPTER 12

Murder on Ireland's Eye?
1852

*'Death was not the result of homicidal drowning or suffocation,
but most probably from a fit resulting from natural causes.'*
DR TAYLOR, *EXPERT ON MEDICAL JURISPRUDENCE*

I n 1847, Spike Island prison was opened, in Cork harbour. It had been a military installation and had then become arguably the worst gaol in Britain. The 1857 annual report into the improvement of prison discipline noted that convicts were at work there on fortifications, and the diet was very poor. But most staggering of all is their table of statistics for 1854: from a total of 2,290 convicts, around 172 were daily sick and 241 had died. Those figures are outrageous by any standards. The Fenian John Mitchel was there before transportation and he was a witness to the disgusting regime. But there was another prisoner there at that awful and brutal period of prison history, and he was not a political prisoner. He was artist William Burke Kirwan, and he

Howth, from an old postcard. Author's collection

was there for the crime of murder – something he almost certainly did not commit.

Judge Bodkin, author of one of the classic works on Irish trials, had access to records, witness statements and scientific experts when he wrote his book in 1918, and he makes a convincing argument for a wrongful conviction.

This complex story of a mysterious death began when Kirwan and his wife, Sarah Maria, set off for a day on the island of Ireland's Eye in 1852. They lived at 11 Merrion Square and they had been married for twelve years; Maria was a good swimmer and everyone knew she loved bathing in the sea. That day, the couple took a boat out to the island and asked to be picked up by the boatmen at eight that evening. They had often been to the island before, so they knew it well. That day they took her bathing dress, water and food and of course, Kirwan's sketchbook. It seems clear that they were going to enjoy their separate pursuits but then eat and chat together as well.

A couple called Brue also went to the island that day but they returned to the mainland earlier. Before eight, several people heard cries coming from the island; the time was about a quarter to eight and several cries were heard. The listeners agreed that the location of the cries was from a place called Long Hole. Then, when the boat left Howth to collect the

Ireland's Eye, from Five Years in Ireland, 1895. Author's collection

Kirwans, they found Kirwan distressed, saying he had not seen his wife since the time earlier when there had been a shower.

The boatmen and Kirwan searched widely for Maria but with no success; then, as it was becoming dark, she was seen, wearing a white dress, lying on her back on a rock by the Long Hole. Her bathing dress was drawn up under her and when they went to look at her, they found that her dress was dry. The tide had receded. A detail at that time was important later – the fact

Merrion Square, where Kirwan had a home. The author

that the men could not find her clothes but Kirwan did. He appeared to go straight to them. The boatmen agreed that, after some time passed and they had taken their boat around to Long Hole to collect the body, Kirwan was most distressed. The body of poor Maria was wrapped and taken to Howth.

Sandymount, where his other family lived. The author

It was noticed at the inquest that there were cuts on her face and eyelid and also on a breast, which was bleeding at the time she was recovered. But the verdict was simply 'found drowned' and she was buried in Glasnevin cemetery.

Then the troubles began for Kirwan. His situation was the origin: the fact that he had another woman and a family of seven children. His mistress lived in Sandymount; she was Mary Kenny and they had been together for a long time. The scandal-mongers said he had been deluding his real wife all those years and leading a disgusting double life. So intense did all this become that the supposed motive emerged and the police acted. Kirwan was charged and arrested and had to face a Grand Jury.

It was a very high-profile case, a sensation in fact: before the trial: as Bodkin wrote, 'The galleries and the seats in the body of the court were densely crowded with an assembly amongst which we observed several ladies.' Everyone wanted a clear view of the prisoner as he came to the dock, and he was reported to have been very much in command of his emotions, a man in his early thirties, smartly dressed in black, and with dark hair and eyes. His demeanour was sober and solemn. A report at the time said he always had a 'calm and collected' stance through all the proceedings. The judges were Judge Crampton and Baron Greene, and Mr Smyly led the prosecution.

Kirwan's life was described, including his double life, and one can imagine the gasps as it was stated that he had lived with both women for twelve years, while earning his living as 'artist and anatomical draughtsman'. He was shown to have spent most of his time with Mary Kenny and the statement made which must have carried the main purport of the moral outrage was: 'There is nothing in the evidence to show when, if ever, wife or mistress became aware of each other's existence, though there is strong ground for believing that each knew about the other from the first.' Statements such as that made by Mr Bridgeford, owner of the Sandymount house, did not help Kirwan's cause. He said, 'Mr Kirwan lived in one of four houses in Spafield of which I am the landlord. He resided there for about four years. I saw a woman whom I always supposed to be his wife. I saw children in the house. I have notes from the woman...and I think she signed herself 'Theresa'.

Evidence and testimony then gathered: a man with a detailed

map of the island knew about the tides and the levels of the water at Long Hole were timed to link to Kirwan's statements about being either with or away from his wife. These seemed to tally well. Then the marital behaviour of the couple was described by a witness with whom they lodged at Howth: the landlady said she had heard Kirwan say 'I'll finish you' and also she had heard Maria say 'Leave me alone'. When we add to this the account of the body and those mysterious cuts and bites, we can see how matters turned very black for the artist.

But for the defence there were equally strong statements to the contrary regarding their life together. One deposition stated that 'I never knew the prisoner and his wife to disagree except on one occasion; I do not know what caused them to disagree, but I always knew them to live happily together.' When talk escalated though, fine detail lifted into a dark area of suspicion, as when the boatman Patrick Nagle said he thought that Kirwan carried what was known as a 'slick stick' – a cane with a sword inside the tube. This proved to be uncertain, and a mere piece of gossip, but it added fuel to the flames.

As to the wounds, the description was that there was a sheet under her back and she had her bathing clothes on, and that there was a cut under her right eye and scratches on her cheek. These marks could have been made by any sharp instrument, even by a pin, it was said, they were so small. Later, when it was too late to save the man, an expert on crabs showed that one particular species was the likely culprit.

It has to be said that the reports by four boatmen of Kirwan's behaviour on that horrendous day suggest that he was distraught and utterly emotionally wrecked. They said he shouted out her name and held her body in grief. In fact, as one witness said, he almost lost his own life, so reckless was he with the shock. The witness said:

Mr Kirwan was very near being killed himself that evening when the body was found. If I had not called and caught him he would have gone over the rock; if he took a step further he would certainly have been killed. A horse would have been killed if it fell then.

The crucially important issue for the defence to sort out was the matter of the manner of death: the main spin given to the information gleaned was that Maria had an attack of epilepsy while in the water – or at least some kind of seizure, perhaps even caused by her having a full stomach. The surgeon questioned was George Hatchel. He said that the cause of death was 'asphyxia or stoppage of respiration'. He also thought that there had been 'constriction of some kind' applied to her.

The defence had to argue against that or they would lose. They tried the 'full stomach' line of thought and that led nowhere, so the supposition of her having an epileptic fit was then voiced. The important point here was that the screams heard could have been related to such a fit. Also, the statement was then made about the crab bites. The coroner said that in his years of experience in that job, he had seen crab bites like that before. Things seemed to be looking up for Kirwan at that point. Witnesses pointed out that people with epilepsy could scream several times in the course of a fit, and the crab bites were likely.

But the prosecution painted a bleak and terrifying picture of a killing:

If he succeeded in forcing her under the water, notwithstanding her fruitless struggles, with all her youthful energy against his superior strength, might they (the shouts) not have been fainter, agonizing, dying shrieks, which both men and women swore they had heard from the mainland growing fainter and fainter?

After half an hour, the jury returned a verdict of guilty. But that was after the chairman had said to the judge that there was not the remotest chance of them agreeing; the judge had said that they must be locked up for the night without food – so they reached a decision.

Kirwan's statement, before the sentence was passed, was a clear and convincing account of the events of that day. He and his wife had parted, him sketching and she bathing. He even described the sketch he had made – something done to catch the light at a specific time (and the police had these sketches as proof). Then he explained his wet feet by saying he had walked through grass after the shower of rain that had fallen – not from standing in water while he took the life of his wife.

But Judge Crampton painted a terrible picture of a brutal murder in his summing up and then passed the sentence of death. Kirwan said:

> *Convinced as I am that my hopes in this world are at an end, I do most solemnly declare in the presence of this court, and before the God before whom I expect soon to stand, that I had neither act nor part nor knowledge of my late wife's death, and I state further that I never treated her unkindly, as her own mother can testify.*

The death sentence was commuted to penal servitude for life by Lord Eglinton, and so Kirwan was sent to Spike Island. He survived the harsh regime and we know that he was released on 3 March 1879, and the stipulation of the release was that he had to live 'outside the British dominions' from that day on.

Judge Bodkin was utterly convinced of Kirwan's innocence, and it is hard to disagree with that judgement. In fact, Bodkin had a personal memory that is entirely pertinent to this famous case:

> *As I was walking one morning along the sea wall to Blackrock, I saw a young man bathing. He had scarcely entered the water when he threw up his hands, screamed violently and fell into a fit. I dragged him out at no greater cost than wet clothes, the water was not more than two feet deep, and I succeeded by friction in completely restoring him. It is no wonder that I found it easy to believe a similar fatality happening to Mrs Kirwan.*

That is why my chapter has a question mark, and as a coda to the tale, it has to be said that Dr Taylor, eminent expert in jurisprudence, has written: 'so far as the appearance of the body was concerned, there is an entire absence of proof that death was the result of violence at the hands of another person...'.

CHAPTER 13

The James Spollen Trial
1857
'It is a terrible thing to be in the hands of a female tiger.'
JAMES SPOLLEN

On Christmas Day 1856, Mr Michael George Harrison was 'turned out of the dock' in court, as there was 'not a particle of evidence' to link him to a murder that had been headline news in the Dublin papers for weeks. The cashier at the Broadstone terminus of the Midland Great Western Railway had been cruelly murdered in his office and a great deal of money stolen.

There had been all kinds of speculation about the circumstances of the killing, as it had all the ingredients of a classic 'locked room' whodunit – except that this was for real. Mr Samuel Little had been a very orderly and well regulated worker, staying late in the office to finish the day's accounts when other employees had left for home at five in the evening. On 13 November 1856 he was working late when someone entered his room, which was locked from the inside, and brutally battered him to death, then cut his throat and damaged his spine to ensure that he would not come round and incriminate them.

Little was a model worker, keeping his mother and sister from his income, and being extremely

Frontispiece to the Trial of James Spollen, *1857.*
Author's collection

TRIAL

OF

JAMES SPOLLEN,

FOR THE MURDER

OF

MR. GEORGE SAMUEL LITTLE,

AT THE BROADSTONE TERMINUS

OF THE

MIDLAND GREAT WESTERN RAILWAY, IRELAND,

AUGUST 7TH, 8TH, 10TH & 11TH, 1857.

DUBLIN:
EDWARD J. MILLIKEN, 15, COLLEGE GREEN.
Price One Shilling.

conscientious. He was described by one associate as 'a quiet, amiable, pleasing man and as unassuming a creature as ever breathed'. He had been promoted to cashier just a few months before this attack and was universally liked. It was his duty to receive and process all incomes, including cash from a docket system, in operation because there were different journeys and fares involved in the railway system – some travellers going on to cross the Irish Sea and go to London for instance. Then there were fees involve in transporting cattle. He also received 'surplus money' which was the profit from business transactions rather than from fares.

On the evening of the attack, not long after he had arranged for a key to be made so that he could lock his office door from the inside, his assistant, young Mr Chamberlain, had gone home at five and Little had stayed on. The timing of the attack indicated that the killer knew something of the railway affairs because it was a day on which there would be far more cash in the office than usual. As was explained later in court:

> *I state to you heavy business because the receipts of that Thursday morning were unusually heavy. Tuesday was the day of the great fair at Mullingar, and on those days the receipts from Mullingar and other stations connected with the removal of cattle were very considerable, so that on Thursday, 13 November, Mr Little necessarily had in his hands a more than usual sum of money…*

In fact, it was calculated that he had handled several hundred pounds. His office was close to some rooms occupied by a few families, and one of these, the people called Gunnings, knew his working hours. On the night of the murder, Mrs Gunning saw a light from his office and went to try the door. That was at around seven o'clock and there was no response or reply when she rattled the handle of the locked door. Either the murderer was in the room at the time or Little was working and wanted to be left alone; yet it was odd that he did not speak to Mrs Gunning.

The geography of the station at Broadstone becomes important in the case now. The next morning, young Chamberlain came and waited at the office door, unable to

Old postcard showing Broadstone terminus. Author's collection

enter. Then after some time, Little's sister arrived, very worried that her brother had not been home the night before. A member of staff called Brophy forced entry by going though a roof and then a side window. It was he who discovered the body of Little. In court, the scene was described by the Attorney General:

> *When Brophy got into the office the first object that met his sight was the mangled body of Mr. Little. He found him lying upon his face... his right hand under him, and his left hand extended and open... the murderer had struck him down, having possibly managed to come and strike the fatal blow from the side, as the unhappy man was probably sitting at his table. He was lying in a pool of blood...*

It is hard to believe, but the first report of this is that it was a case of suicide. When we consider the fact that Little had his throat cut from side to side and indeed that the vertebrae of his spinal column were sliced, the idea of suicide is ridiculous, but all this served to delay the investigation, as also did the search for the weapon or weapons used.

Then, on 26 June 1857, came the breakthrough. The papers reported that the wife of James Spollen had gone to talk to

Inspector Guy; some got the information in a garbled way, even having his name as Joseph, but what emerged was that this painter and handyman who worked for the railway and lived very near to the offices and sheds, was arrested and charged. Mrs Spollen had spilled the beans and told the police that Spollen had told her he had done the murder. He was taken to Frederick Lane police station and the readers of the papers at last had a description of him:

The prisoner is about 43 years of age, about five feet eight inches high, of sandy complexion and wears large whiskers. His face is exceedingly pale and he has lost his right eye. He was brought over from England at the time of the erection of the zinc roof on the Broadstone terminus about the year 1845 and has remained in the employment of the railway company as a painter.

He was moved to Sackville Place station ready for the magistrates the next morning. What then happened was that Mrs Mary Spollen became the centre of media attention as she was visibly active in demanding repentance from her husband, and she was revealing more and more about the murder as the days passed. She said that her suspicions had first been aroused when he came home later than usual, bringing with him a bucket in which there was a large sum of money. She also related how he had entered and left by the roof. The Spollens' house was not far from the cattle platform. The wall running along the side of the platform at the western side of the railway, rose to a height of five feet above the walking level and then there was a boundary wall and beyond that there was a small cavity in which, eventually, the money stolen was mostly traced.

Constable Donelly was the man who found the stash; he managed to get partly into a tiny chamber with an entrance of around three feet and there was a small tub, and under some red lead there were bags of silver; the various stores of cash were divided into the categories in which they were handled by Little. Over £200 was recovered. Mrs Spollen then gave police some clothes which had been worn by her husband – the clothes she said he had been wearing when he did the awful deed. The details of his work then were explained more fully; he was hired to work on a leak between a glass and iron roof, and then his son was also employed after his father's trial period. Earlier in the search, because the Spollen house was near, it had been searched by police three times but nothing of any relevance or significance was ever found.

On 30 June, the final elusive piece of material evidence was found: this was the key to Little's door. A workhouse boy found this in a heap of mud where Mrs Spollen had said her husband had thrown it. There had been an extensive police operation, as *The Times* reported: 'The little river Bradogue was explored in every part from the boundary of the railway to the extreme end of the North Union workhouse garden… Archways and lagging were taken away to facilitate the search…'

But before he appeared at the trial, Mrs Spollen had one more major card to play in making sure that the world knew how supposedly evil her husband was. She now told the police that he had tried to poison her. The report at the time said that her children had gone to fetch a doctor, she was so ill, and the doctor had found her in bed 'suffering in acute agony from spasms in the stomach and violent retching'. A paralysis affected her and she had to have special treatment to recover. Mary Spollen made a complex documentary narrative of her husband's life and brought in dimensions of fear, paranoia and sheer drama to paint him black. As the trial drew near, it was reported that she was as active as ever in recreating her husband's actions: 'Mrs Spollen was engaged during part of yesterday indicating to the police the places where she thought her husband was likely to have concealed the missing £50 and the search was continued up to an advanced hour but without success…' There was even a revelation from Mary Spollen that a razor belonging to her husband, given to him by a friend, was a likely weapon.

Spollen was moved to Richmond bridewell and then came the trial. It was long and complicated, and there was extensive explanation and discussion of the statements made by members of Spollen's family, but in the end, the evidence was circumstantial. There was nothing to definitely prove that he had been there on that night and had done the murder. Even worse for the prosecution was the high media interest and the danger of prejudicial views in the jury. In fact at the beginning of proceedings, several members of the jury were challenged and then replaced.

In the conclusion and summing up, the judge was at a loss for any confident statement to be made, saying to the jury, 'if you come to the conclusion that it is impossible that the children of that man could be conspirators to take away the author of their being.... If you come to the conclusion that the razor was his...if above all, you come to the conclusion that he said he was with his family... he was at the roof of the smithy [adjoining the station] it will be for you, on your consciences, to say whether that can be...' In other words, this was a classic template of that criminal trial in which there were very large doubts and many speculative theories which could not be upheld with confidence.

The Clerk of the Crown asked the chairman of the jury the important question and the reply was 'Not guilty'. James Spollen spoke and in a 'broken manner' he said:

> *My conviction was fixed that I stood before twelve of my countrymen... I thought they would impartially take my case into consideration and they have done so. It is not for me to commence to praise myself, but I have been brought here in a wrongful way... I always liked the man and I loved the woman but it is a dreadful thing to be in the hands of a female tiger...*

Spollen walked free, but that was not the end of it; he was still charged with the theft, if not the murder, and there is a tone of disbelief and frustration in the newspaper report of that outcome: on 27 October that year, a final paragraph relating to the Spollen saga appeared in *The Times*:

> *The Crown has sustained another defeat in the attempt to make James Spollen amenable to justice. The commission was opened today before Barons Greene and Richards, and the latter having delivered his charge, the grand jury retired to consider the several bills before them. After an absence of about two hours, they returned into court and the foreman announced that they had found 'no bill' in the case of James Spollen, charged with robbery of the late Mr Little.*

James Spollen was discharged from custody. It is splitting legal hairs, but in a paper given by experts in jurisprudence it was stated that Spollen would have been better served by a verdict of 'Not proven' if Irish law had indeed had such an option. The author of that opinion said that because Spollen would have better benefited in terms of public opinion.

We have to feel that Spollen, no doubt enjoying a quiet beer and a huge smile of relief that he was free, would have cared little for such definitions and verdicts. He must have gloried in the feeling that they hadn't pinned anything on him at all, in spite of Mary's vigour and resolve in creating a documentary history of the whole supposed crime.

CHAPTER 14

Libel and Dr Wilde
1864

'When you are as old as I am, young man, you will know that
there is only one thing worth living for, and that is sin...'
LADY WILDE

Admirers of the work of Oscar Wilde will always think of his trial, arrest and imprisonment in Reading Gaol as a central aspect of his life; it typifies his tendency to make enemies, to stir things up around him, and to thrive on dissent and disagreement. The heart of his best work is a critique of many of the moral values of his time. But perhaps not so well known is the turbulent life of his father, Sir William Wilde, the famous Dublin doctor. The most sensational affair in his often scandalous life is one that involved a court case, and in many ways, the plaintiff was the person on trial.

William Wilde and his wife, Jane (who was a writer herself, known as 'Esperanza'), were major figures in Dublin life and culture in the 1860s. He was a famous specialist in eye, nose and throat medicine and his knowledge and skills were widely admired. But he was also something of a womaniser, and in an atmosphere of what one biographer calls the 'Regency permissiveness' of the time, William Wilde acquired a reputation of a man who liked a good time and whose morals were not perhaps what they should have been.

Although Lady Wilde was clearly tolerant of her husband's small misdemeanours, when it came to a libel case against her, things became very difficult. It all began when a young woman called Mary Travers, who had been a patient of Sir William, began to spread rumours about her being raped by him while under chloroform. The incident had allegedly happened two years before this gossip appeared – and that is a strange fact in itself – and it seems more than accidental that she began to make trouble at the time when Wilde had been knighted in 1864

Two views of Sir William Wilde's home on Merrion Square. The author

and when Lady Wilde was becoming a literary celebrity in Ireland.

Travers had been a patient of Wilds since 1854, but was claiming that she had been 'ruined' in 1862; she wrote letters to newspapers with veiled allegations and even wrote a satire on the Wildes called 'Dr and Mrs Quilp'. But it was when Lady Wilde wrote a letter to Mary Travers' father that Mary took legal action. It read:

TOWER, BRAY May 6th.
Sir, you may not be aware of the disreputable conduct of your daughter at Bray where she consorts with all the low newspaper boys of the place, employing them to disseminate offensive placards in which my name is given, and also tracts in which she makes it appear that she has had an intrigue with Sir William Wilde... I think it right to inform you, as no

threat of additional insult shall ever extort money from our hands…

Mary Travers found out about this letter and sued Lady Wilde for libel; she took out a civil action, and had it been a criminal trial there would have been all kinds of unspeakable scrutiny and scandal, with Travers being very unlikely to have her man convicted, as there had been a gap of over two years since the alleged rape. In addition to that, the woman had acquired the reputation of being a fantasist and her statements were often laughably bizarre. But her counsel was Isaac Butt, a notable character around the city and very well known. That fact alone attracted a great deal of interest.

The story of the trial has been somewhat exaggerated in the pages of Frank Harris's book on Oscar Wilde, but at least Harris points out the strange nature of the events. The case was heard before Chief Justice Monahan in the Court of Common Pleas, and Mary Travers was claiming £2,000 damages for Lady Wilde's libel. Because Lady Wilde was married, her husband was part of the action, as a co-defendant for conformity.

In her writings and squibs on Wilde, Travers had written, 'It is sad to think that in the nineteenth century a lady must not venture into a physician's study without being accompanied by a bodyguard to protect her.' She had published verses in local papers and written letters to *Saunders Newsletter*, so Wilde's defence had plenty of material there to use. But what emerged was a long and ambiguous relationship between Wilde and Travers, going back to his first treatment of her, when he cured her of a hearing problem.

Travers came to Wilde when she was just nineteen and partially deaf. He cured her and instead of the relationship ending there, a friendship developed. Wilde had written letters, given her gifts and even paid for a voyage to Australia for her. She had even been to dinner with the Wildes. There developed a voyeuristic interest in Travers' body: it was explained that she had a scar on her neck and that when treated by Wilde, she had to kneel down on a hassock before him. Wilde had also pared a painful corn she had. The narrative created by the defence was being compiled as one suggestive of a sensual and very tempting doctor-patient relationship.

When Mary Travers entered the witness box the court was treated to a graphic and detailed account of what Travers wanted to present as a seduction and as an act of an older man (and a professional) taking advantage of a simple young girl. Frank Harris summarises the tone and content very strongly:

> *In October, 1862, it appeared Lady Wilde was not at the house at Merrion Square but was away at Bray... Dr. Wilde was alone in the house. Miss Travers called, and was admitted into Dr. Wilde's study. He put her on her knees before him and bared her back, pretending to examine the burn; he fondled her too much and pressed her to him... Somehow or other his hand got entangled in a chain at her neck.... she declared that she lost consciousness.*

The allegation was that Wilde had applied chloroform and then raped her while she was unconscious.

The judge asked Travers if she knew that she had been violated and she replied 'Yes.' But there were complications and confusions; she had not been sure of the day when this was supposed to have happened, and she admitted that she had asked Wilde for money on several occasions. Of course, after the supposed assault, she kept on going back to Wilde's study. She even claimed that he had repeated the assault. The most damning event on her fabricated tale was when she was asked about the chloroform. She became confused and was not sure whether he had used a rag or a handkerchief, despite saying that she had seen him throw it into a fire. She could not even distinguish the smell of chloroform in court, and simply broke down.

Frank Harris commented on how Lady Wilde, when she had her turn in the box, was welcomed and applauded by the gallery, and he thought that even the judge and jury had been impressed by her. But Lady Wilde did not escape without some searching questions; she was asked if she hated Miss Travers and she replied that she did not hate anyone. Then the crucially important question was put – why did she not respond to the first letter she received from Travers telling her of her husband's conduct? She simply said that she had no interest in the matter.

Naturally, this whole affair could have had very serious consequences for William Wilde, and some writers have suggested that after the fiasco he was a broken man, but there is little to support that view. Chief Justice Monahan made the telling remark that had the trial been a criminal one, then no-one would have believed Miss Travers.

Isaac Butt was a smart character though, and he did well for Travers in a difficult situation. He made the point that the defence they had all witnessed was practically a justification of the libel. In the end, the whole point was whether or not there had been a nasty seduction, an exploitation of a vulnerable young woman in the hands of a respectable and well-liked medical man. Wilde never went into the witness box and that was seen by some as very strange. He was actually the defendant, even though the libel was principally directed at Mary Wilde.

In the end it was an ironical verdict. The jury retired for two hours and on their return they awarded Mary Travers damages of one farthing and noted that the sum should carry some costs. Frank Harris wrote in response: 'In other words they rated Miss Travers' virtue at the very lowest coin of the realm, while insisting that Sir William Wilde should pay a couple of thousands of pounds for having seduced her.' Wilde was supported by the prestigious journal of the British Medical Association, *The Lancet*, and just to reinforce how crazy Travers could be, after a journal in Ireland had written a piece in favour of Wilde in the affair, she took libel proceedings against them. Obviously, she failed.

Yet such turbulent and juicy affairs tend to persist and also they circulate in the popular culture, and Richard Ellmann, the biographer of Oscar Wilde, has

Isaac Butt, who acted for Miss Travers, from Vanity Fair, *1910.* Author's collection

pointed out that Oscar would have heard this rhyme while he was at Trinity College:

An eminent oculist lives in the Square,
His skill is unrivalled, his talent is rare,
And if you will listen I'll certainly try
To tell how he opened Miss Travers's eye.

Nothing in this scandalous case affected his practice and reputation. His base in the city at Merrion Square has a plaque to his memory today, and in his own time, in 1873, the Royal Academy of Ireland gave him the Cunningham Gold Medal, its most important award.

The Royal College of Surgeons in Ireland today. The author

CHAPTER 15

A Chronicle of Victorian Murder
1870–1900
'I was very nervous when I was asked to go to Ireland.'
JAMES BERRY, HANGMAN

The prisons and their execution suites were busy in Dublin and the county of Dublin throughout the nineteenth century. When it came to murders and death sentences, the hangmen had to cross the Irish Sea from England: Ireland did not have its own hangman. James Berry, the Bradford executioner, was the one hangman who recorded the nature of going to Ireland to do a hanging in the nineteenth century: he said 'I was very nervous when I had to go to Ireland, and I asked my wife to go with me to look after me.' Once, going to Tralee, he was met by a detective who told him that another officer had refused to do the job, saying, 'I would rather give up my position than handle the ribbons for the hangman of England.'

So when we read about the murder cases in Dublin in these years when the trade of hangman was steadily being more professionalised, we have to recall that Englishmen were called in, and clearly, the situation, for obvious political reasons, would be fraught with tension and danger. But these hangmen were certainly busy: William Marwood from Lincolnshire introduced the long drop method which made the business rather more humane and swift, and he is perhaps most well-known because he it was who hanged the Phoenix Park murderers.

Some of the Dublin killings in these years were in the lowest, most deprived areas, such as the simple, straightforward murder of an old lady, Bridget Knight, in 1893, by teenager Edward Leigh. She was found stabbed to death at her home, and there was such revulsion at this that the jury's feeling that there should be mercy applied on account of the prisoner's youth was ignored. He was hanged on 9 June. In Dublin, convicts from the city were hanged at Newgate in Green Street and Dublin

How the Victorians saw the Irish, from Punch, *1846.* Punch

county killers were hanged at Kilmainham.

Most killings were unremarkable, such as the attack on Bernard Cox, an insurance agent, in 1893. He was attacked by James Reilly at Stepaside, beaten to death with an iron bar. Yorkshireman Thomas Scott was on duty for both Leigh and Reilly. Scott did not need to have an assistant with him.

A more unusual case, and one that in some ways went against the rules and conventions, was that of Joseph Poole, who was a Fenian who shot an informer, John Kenny, in July 1882. Kenny was about to reveal details of a police killing and while he was staying in lodgings in Seville Place, Poole, shot him dead. Although there were witnesses, none of them said a word, but

The Lord Mayor of Dublin goes to work in prison,
from the Illustrated Penny Paper, *1855.* Author's collection

his brother-in-law eventually gave evidence against him. What was remarkable here was that Poole was hanged by a man who was not on a list of executioners – someone called Jones. As one might expect, the affair was botched and Poole did not die quickly.

Of all the murders in these years, the story of Peter Stafford and his failed alibi provide most scaffold drama. Stafford killed a man and claimed his innocence, giving an alibi, but executioner James Berry was soon on his way to Dublin again. It was a tough assignment: Berry went to Kilmainham and he found that Mrs Stafford with her child and her brother, had been to have a last visit to the condemned man and emotions were whipped up to breaking point around the gaol. The wife tried again to see her husband on the morning of the hanging, but the governor would have none of that.

It was a desperately terrifying scene in the death cell as

Stafford fought hard against being pinioned; he had two priests with him, Fathers Kennedy and Byrne, but the man fought with such resolution that several warders had to help Berry with the job. But at least Berry did his work well, giving the man a very speedy exit. With a drop of six feet six inches, the man fell and died instantaneously. Stafford had screamed, 'Lord have mercy on me! God forgive me my sins!' But the fact is that he had killed a man in cold blood, merely over a farming dispute.

Naturally, the 1882 Phoenix Park murders brought about some major changes in law: the Crimes Acts of 1882 and 1887 brought about more repression. After all, a gang had murdered the Chief Secretary for Ireland, Lord Frederick Cavendish, and his under-secretary in daylight while they were walking in the park. Four men had leapt from a cab and stabbed them to death. The 'Irish Invincibles' as they called themselves, sent black-bordered cards to the Dublin papers.

Phoenix Park in 1878. The Graphic

Brady had gone with one group, and Curley with others, after a planning meeting at *Wrenn's Tavern* near Dublin Castle. They agreed to split up and decide on where the attack would take place. They had made sure that they had correctly identified Harry Burke, so there would be no mistakes. As they were gathering in the park, there was almost a very big problem for them, because a Police Superintendent called Mallon was going to the park to meet one of his contacts, and he met a plain-clothes detective who warned him of an attempt on his life; Mallon left, so the coast was clear for the assassins.

Another turn of fate for the victims was that Cavendish had been offered a ride instead, but insisted that he walk with Burke. As Cavendish was only just in place as the Secretary there were things to talk through and a stroll obviously seemed a leisurely way to do that. But they were walking to an appointment with death. After a man called Timothy Kelly had advanced and knifed Cavendish, the gang were soon upon them, with Brady cutting Burke's throat in the assault. They made their escape, hoping to drive around the city and approach Dublin from another entrance, thus making a platform for some kind of alibi, but the detective had seen a number of them and would later identify them. The first move in cracking the gang and charging them was possible after a driver broke down and told the tale. The rest is scaffold history.

Once again, the English hangman came to Dublin: this time it was William Marwood. Sixteen of the Invincibles were arrested and five were hanged; James Carey turned state's evidence. The Invincibles were a splinter group from the Fenians; the murders shocked everyone – in England and in Ireland, and had a profound effect on public opinion with regard to militant nationalist action.

Joseph Brady was executed on 14 May, sentenced to death by Mr Justice O'Brien. Brady had plunged a long knife into the back of the Secretary, Harry Burke, and then stabbed Lord Frederick Cavendish. After that came Daniel Curley, a superintendent of the Invincibles, and the man who appears to have been the planner behind the group.

Not all Dublin murders of these years provide us with closure and a neat end to the story. For instance, one of the most tantalising scraps in the contemporary reports is about a

The centre of British administration: Dublin Castle. The author

mystery man called Walsh who was arrested in Shropshire for a Dublin murder and all the reporter could say was that 'the Irish police are very reticent on the matter and will say nothing when pressed'.

Then we have, in complete contrast to the Phoenix Park murders, the story of Andrew Carr, who was a discharged army pensioner. He walked up to a police constable in Bull Lane, in a slum area of the city, and said, 'I am just after murdering a woman in a house in Bull Lane by cutting her throat and if you don't believe me, look at my hands.' The man was slightly drunk, the constable recalled; he saw blood on the man's hands and a deep cut. Carr went on the tell the officer that he had recently been in the 37th Regiment.

They went to the house, and the newspaper report at the time explained the scene:

The constable proceeded to the house, which is in a most dilapidated and filthy condition, the windows and balusters broken, and the stairs in a rickety state. He entered a wretched back room on the third storey, which contained no furniture except two wooden stools and a few cracked cups on the mantelpiece, and in an inner closet found a straw pallet on which the murdered woman lay.

Carr said he had gone upstairs with the woman, who was called Margaret Murphy, killed her, and gone outside again. He said it was an attack in revenge for something she had done months before.

In court, there was a plea of insanity but that failed. But there is a gruesome and gut-wrenching end to this murder story: Carr was sentenced to hang, and at Richmond Gaol at the scaffold the calculation of the drop had been done wrongly: it was a fourteen foot drop but he was a very heavy man and the sudden jerk as the bolt was withdrawn severed his head from his body.

CHAPTER 16

Lured to Death
1884

'He had been half-beaten, half kicked to death…'
THE TIMES

I t took some time to get Peter Wade, a labourer from Rathfarnham, to trial. He was charged before a magistrate with murder on 29 October 1883 and in those days trial and sentences were done within a space of ten days if the case was clear and the jury sure. But Wade must have thought the omens were good when his trial at the Green Street Commission Court in Dublin was deferred. The counsel for Wade asked for a delay because, as he put it, there had not been sufficient time since professional assistance was assigned to make enquiries. The Crown was busy enough, as there was a nasty Westmeath murder to sort out.

But on 15 December he stood in court. Wade was just twenty-three, and he was working as a labourer. The charge was that he had killed an old man aged seventy, Patrick Quinn, a gardener living with his wife at Knocklion. A few days before the death, Wade had come to the Quinn's house and asked to see the old man. He told Mrs Quinn that the matter was a private one, but she was slightly suspicious, saying that there were no secrets between herself and her husband. But Wade stayed hanging around the place and when he did get to talk to Quinn, they were busy with a discussion of another man called Malone.

The two men seemed to argue about Malone: Wade said he was a rogue and Quinn contradicted him. They talked about Malone leaving his holding without paying his rent. There was some bad feeling, but at that point Mrs Quinn was not sure exactly what that was; but she did have a very good look at Wade of course, and that was important later.

On the night of the 27 October, just after that meeting, Wade returned. The men spoke, sat down and had some tea. According to one report, there would have been no cause for concern then, and shortly after that they walked out together. But it was not long after they left the house that neighbours heard screams and in a short while, Quinn's body was found. But another story on the case makes far more sinister reading. That account states that Wade waited outside Quinn's house waiting for the old man to come home; when he did come home, Wade asked a friend to go in and lure him out.

A short while after the screams were heard, Quinn was found dead in a lane. He had been half-beaten, half-kicked to death. The wounds on his head were horrific, so savage had the attack been. The only talk about the case at the time was about Quinn finding a job for Malone, and Wade had taken against him for that, such was his capacity for enmity and hatred.

The hunt for Wade did not last long, even though he had tried to disguise himself, very feebly, because he had merely clipped his moustache. But there were bloodstains on his clothes when he was arrested, and some hair that matched his was found near the body. Clearly, Peter Wade was not the smartest of individuals. Mary Quinn, of course, described Wade clearly and confirmed that when she saw him on his first visit, he had had a moustache. He was well known to the local police, and Constable John Burke stated that he had known Wade for nine years.

Wade was arrested while in his bed and taken away for questioning. When it came to him putting together some kind of story in defence, Wade said that he was not the killer, but that he had sent to decoy Quinn out of the town so that others could lie in wait for him. It did him no good at all and the jury found him guilty of wilful murder.

By 14 January, after an application for reprieve to the Under Secretary, a Dr Kaye from the Under Secretary's office wrote to Wade's solicitor with the news that after a full consideration of all the circumstances of the case, his Excellency has felt it to be his painful duty to decide that the law must take its course. Wade had no hope, and he wrote this last letter from Kilmainham:

> I cannot leave this world and face my God without clearing the people I told Sergeant Seads about. They know nothing about what happened and had no hand in it. All I said in that

statement was wrong. I hope the men I mentioned in my statement will forgive me. I should like it published and their characters cleared. Fully expecting in a few hours to meet my God, I declare what I am now saying is true.

This was witnessed by some of the men who would see him die the next day - Governor J Leslie Beers and Martin Walsh, Chief Warder.

On 15 January he was hanged. Before death, he had spiritual support from Reverend Monsignor Kennedy and Reverend O'Reilly, who heard his confession and administered the sacrament. Wade was in the hands of a very experienced executioner, Yorkshireman Bartholomew Binns, a man who kept a shop in Dewsbury when he was not plying his second trade of hangman. He gave Wade a speedy death, there being just two minutes between the first pinioning restraint and the man swinging dead on the noose. In other words, he died of asphyxia, and very quickly.

But there is a dramatic coda to the story and it is about the widow. Mrs Quinn caught the attention of the papers that day. She had walked all the way from Rathfarnham to Kilmainham to hear the bell toll and then to watch the black flag hoisted when all was finished. She had actually asked to watch Wade die but that request had been refused. She began to cry bitterly when she saw the black flag; but she came through that to tell the press that she was now happy. As *The Times* reported: 'It was a happy sight for her for now she knew that her poor dear husband had been avenged... She had been married 44 years and never had an angry word with her husband all that time. She manifested a very bitter spirit, remained watching the flag for a long time and exclaimed repeatedly, "Oh was not I lucky to be able to identify the murderer!" '

CHAPTER 17

Smotheration in the Monto
c.1890 –1920

*'The combination of soldiery, drink and poverty,
and the sanction of law kept the district flourishing.'*
PETER SOMERVILLE-LARGE

Every city has its red light districts, its slums and its centres of crime. The ancient formula of poverty and deprivation equalling crime is easy to locate in any place where there are large communities in close proximity. In Dublin, what is now Foley Street, was once at the heart of the area known as the 'Monto' – Montgomery Street and Mecklenburgh Street being the real focus of activity. Recent writers such as Frank Hopkins and especially Terry Fagan, have had much to say about the rich, teeming human history there,

'Man walking on Eden Quay' by J J Clarke.
Courtesy of the National Library of Ireland.

particularly in the late Victorian and Edwardian period, when the British Army provided much of the custom for thousands of young girls who had either been attracted by the quick money, knowing the trade, or the more innocent country girls who may have been lured there by the 'madams' thinking they were going into domestic service.

In the 1960s the area achieved the status of being a popular folk song performed by The Dubliners, with the lines:

If you've had your fill of porter
And you can't go any further
Take her up to Monto
Langa-roo.

The origins of Montgomery Street itself are in the lifestyles of the wealthy, in late eighteenth century Dublin when such people as Lord Mountjoy, because Elizabeth Montgomery married Luke Gardiner, Lord Mountjoy at that time, and Dorothea Herbert, living there in that period, wrote of being with her aunt in Mecklenburgh Street when it was a very middle class area. In a directory of 1847, there were many solicitors' offices in and around that street.

It is not really clear why these streets became an area of brothels. One theory is that after Emmet's rebellion there were so many soldiers stationed in the city that more room had to be found for them beyond the barracks in Portland Row that they were accommodated in Mecklenburgh Street and so the custom was there. But equally the shift towards a more seedy area may have come, according to one tradition, after two British regiments were posted to the city after the Crimean War in 1856. Certainly, as the bad reputation grew, changes of name were a ploy to try to lessen the resonance of the name. So Mecklenburgh Street for instance, became Tyrone Street.

Terry Fagan has written a whole book on the Monto, having worked on its history for years. He pointed out in a recent interview that in spite of the reputation of the place as a spot where there was fun, leisure and plenty of drink and sex, there was a dark side, and that lay with the notorious madams of the brothels. He has traced some of the most celebrated ones back to directories in the 1860s, so clearly some of the businesses were 'high class' in both their image and their clients. He points out that there was around 1,600 girls working there at any one time. Although some of the clients were even royalty (Edward VII for instance), for many of the women it was a desperately stressful and miserable life; Fagan notes that girls who became pregnant were more than likely to be thrown out onto the streets.

The most shameful and criminal aspect of the Monto trade was the ruthless treatment of women. It was not unknown for girls who suffered from sexually transmitted disease to be sent to the Lock Hospital and as Fagan says, 'Were often put out of their misery... a favoured method of euthanasia was 'smotheration'. 'The Lock' as it was known, was the Westmoreland Hospital for Incurables, so we can see how the kind of murder Fagan describes could be done at that time with a cloak of supposed 'caring'. If a person went to The Lock it meant they were in oblivion; the place itself was never in the public consciousness, and it depended on charities, and of course it was only fitting that the British army should cough up: the British War Office gave £1,100 for each year between 1899 and 1906. Even today, Dubliners use the phase, 'He's locked' meaning very drunk and therefore in oblivion, out of circulation.

The madams were well organised and knew how to keep their trade thriving; before regiments arrived they delivered business cards to the officers' mess and generally knew about movements and deployments when it suited them to think ahead. But the madams and their women also had to be ready for trouble. One piece of oral history suggests that it was the habit to keep pieces of lead piping behind religious pictures 'in case of trouble'. We have images of the madams through literature as well, as in Oliver St John Gogarty's book, *Tumbling in the Hay* in which he writes of a Mrs Mack who had a 'red brick face on which avarice was written like a hieroglyphic and a laugh like a guffaw in hell'.

The decline came after 1925, when there had been some impact from the Legion of Mary. Before that, there had been some police action, such as the planned raids on the area by Sir John Ross, the Commissioner of Police. Then, a familiar pattern emerged: the places were shut down in the Monto, so the women moved on and were soon an annoyance to the authorities in O'Connell Street and elsewhere. The Monto thrived again for a while after that. Terry Fagan has talked about events such as a murder done on the order of Michael Collins in the Monto: a madam called Betty Cooper's brother was the target and he was shot.

Then along came Frank Duff; he was at first working for the St Vincent de Paul organisation and then his life was changed by a visit to a group of prostitutes, at which meeting he begged them to give up their profession. He heard the argument that has been stated ever since the oldest profession was in existence: if they gave up that work, who would feed them? What work could they do? Duff found a convent that would take them and he also was given a house for them by William Cosgrave.

In 1921, Duff founded the Legion of Mary. It met first in an old shop in Francis Street and steadily grew, eventually having around thirteen million members. But to establish his group, Duff had to confront the madams and of course they were powerful people. History and hard graft effected the victory: Duff and his team persisted in canvassing around the area, and then, politics took a hand because the British army withdrew from Ireland as the new Free State was born. The closures took place with a small payment to the madams (£40 – maybe not so small then).

When Monto was closed in 1925 there were 120 arrests; two madams were arrested, and one, Polly Butler, was given a prison term of six weeks.

Chapter 18

A Fight Over a Play
1907
'Fifty policemen in the aisles exercised a restraining influence.'
David Greene

There are not many times in the history of drama and literature that a work of art causes riots in the streets and in public buildings, but one of those times, and it was a very stirring and worrying event, was in Dublin, and at the very heart of what we now think of as the Irish Literary Renaissance. It had the poet Yeats shouting at the audience and playwright John Synge suffering all kinds of soul-searching stress and unease as his masterpiece seemed to split society apart.

Literature in Ireland has always had that tendency to be political and therefore to be misunderstood; in a country which has had so many invaders, so many internal divisions and such extreme struggles over ideas as well as over land and property, it comes as no surprise to learn that its writers can very easily be defined as somehow falling short of the mark. But in the case of John Synge and his play, *The Playboy of the Western World*, on the surface it seems bizarre that there should have been such hatred and resentment in the public. It is a play in which a son murders a father, or thinks he has, and there is a certain depiction of the West of Ireland peasantry that can be read as highly critical. Yet at the basis of Synge's art there is his fascination with folklore, rural communities and with the language and dialect of parts of the world which have not seen much social change.

To make matters worse, the trouble happened at the Abbey Theatre in Marlborough Street, Dublin. As I write this in 2007, *The Playboy of the Western World* is being performed at that very theatre; there are no riots and no dissent. But the Ireland of 1907 was a very different place, with many more uncertainties, sensitivities and doubts about itself and its direction.

The Abbey Theatre today. The author

John Synge was born in Rathfarnham in 1871. He studied at Trinity College and also at the Royal Irish Academy of Music. For three years after 1899 he lived with the Aran Islanders and

The 'Playboy' – still going strong. The author

developed a strong interest in the history, language and culture of the West of Ireland. This experience was 'material' for his plays and also for his book on the Aran Islands. He became friendly with W B Yeats, who helped and encouraged him, and he was then involved in the founding of the Abbey Theatre. He was never really well, suffering from Hodgkin's Disease, and he was to die just two years after the riots in response to his *Playboy* story.

The theatre was in the habit of keeping new productions under covers, but various people looked at the script, and saw

Synge at work in rehearsals, and there was discussion about the need to do some cuts. Willie Fay wanted some of the more cruel details taken out, and Synge did cut some lines, but not to the satisfaction of Lady Gregory, who wrote in her memoirs that 'I told Synge that the cuts were not enough... I took out many phrases... which, ever since that first production, have not been spoken on our stage.'

Synge agreed to cut some 'bad language' but there was one key passage that stayed in, and it was certain to provoke anger; this was: 'It's Pegeen I'm seeking only, and what I'd care if you brought me a drift of chosen females, standing in their shifts itself, maybe, from this place to the eastern world?' But Synge continued to defend his art on the grounds that his language was only what he had heard spoken. He said he had heard expressions word for word, and that 'the central incident of the Playboy was suggested by an actual occurrence in the west'.

Although there were rumours of possible complaints and some aggressive reactions, there was no overt fear of any trouble on the horizon; an audience primarily made up of nationalists of various shades would be expected to be sympathetic in some ways. But that was a gross miscalculation. The opening night came along, and at first the crowd were quiet, but then the speech about the 'shifts' caused a stir. The audience started hissing and booing. One man wrote after the first performance that Synge was the 'evil genius' of the Abbey Theatre. People tried to comfort the sick and stressed playwright with words such as '...it's better to have the row we had last night than to have your play fizzling out in half-hearted applause'. But there was far worse to come.

With Lady Gregory, who was a joint founder of The Abbey in 1904, Synge decided to call in the police for the second performance; after all the *Irish Times* had made it clear that the play was scandalous, saying, 'what in other respects was a brilliant success' had finally 'an inglorious conclusion'. What really counted though, in terms of whipping up nationalist fervour and old-fashioned morality was the opinion of *The Freeman's Journal* as it supported the moderate nationalist Irish Party under John Redmond, and unfortunately the verdict there was that the play was 'an unmitigated, protracted libel upon Irish peasant men, and worse, upon Irish peasant girlhood.. The blood boils with indignation as one recalls the incidents, expressions, ideas, of his squalid, offensive production, incongruously styled a comedy...'

On the next performance, there were police present by the vestibule door. William Fay, who played the lead role, said that the audience had become 'a veritable mob of howling devils'. The row became a real riot and the crowd were about to storm the stage itself when there was a feat of remarkable fortitude by a call-boy, who grabbed a huge axe and stood before them, saying that he swore by all the saints in the calendar that he would chop the head off the first lad who came over the footlights.'

Fay begged the protesters to go, and promised that they would have their money back; but the crowd yelled, 'Kill the author!' As performances went on regardless, things escalated. The audience stamped their feet and fights broke out. Finally, after the worst responses, there were 500 police called out on duty and a reporter said they were 'as thick as blackberries in September'.

On the Tuesday performance, the great poet, W B Yeats, arrived and tried to act to save the situation, but when he addressed the restless audience that night, he said that the people making the row were philistines, that 'they had no books in their houses' and that they were 'commonplace and ignorant people'. That did not really improve things. He shouted at the audience 'We have put this play before you to be heard and to be judged.. The country that condescends either to bully or to permit itself to be bullied soon ceases to have any fine qualities...'

On Wednesday night there was a fist fight. There were fifty police officers in the aisles, but still there was violence and then later, in the streets, there was a rowdy procession. Matters had to lead to the magistrates' court, and Yeats was there to testify against the offenders, and they were fined ten shillings each. But things settled down by the Friday performance and there was only one arrest then.

As David Greene wrote in his biography of John Synge, 'The most tumultuous event in Dublin theatrical history was over, though the debate over the man who had slain his da was to rage for weeks to come and the riots were to be repeated years later in places as remote from Dublin as New York and Montreal.'

The first inkling of trouble was when Lady Gregory sent a simple telegram to the author with the message: 'Play broke up in disorder at the word shift.' As has been pointed out by various writers, if only Synge had used another word, things might not have got out of hand. But the whole experience did nothing to help his already delicate state of health and he took to his bed with a severe 'flu infection for weeks afterwards.

CHAPTER 19

The Crown Jewels Disappear
1907

'…Sir Arthur Vicars must bear the responsibility.'
J B DOUGHERTY

On the morning of Saturday 6 July 1907, a cleaning lady called Mary Farrell, working at Dublin Castle, was going about her duties and had reached the library when she noticed that the door was unlocked. She had found the same situation three days before that but no action had been taken by Sir Arthur Vicars when it was reported. Vicars was the Ulster King of Arms and he was responsible not merely for the security of the library and rooms around, but for something far more important – the Insignia of the Most Illustrious Order of St Patrick, otherwise known as the Irish 'Crown Jewels'.

These were in a safe in the library because when the safe had been taken to the Castle from a bank vault, in order to be kept at the Office of Arms, it was found that the safe was too large to be taken in, so it was placed in the library of the Bedford Tower. Not only was it a solid safe, it was also in a position where soldiers and police officers would always be in close proximity, so it must have seemed a secure place to store such valuables. How wrong could the men responsible have been – because later on after the cleaner made the second report on the sixth of the month, William Stivey, who was an assistant to Vicars, went to the safe and found that it was unlocked and that the jewels had gone.

The jewels were the insignia of a group formed by George III in 1783, as an Irish form of the famous Scottish Order of the Thistle. The jewels had been made in London by a company called Rundell and Bridge and the glory of the collection comprised two items: a star and badge of the Order of St Patrick. The statutes and rules of the order had only recently been revised – just two years previously – and the Office of

The Record Tower, within the Castle. The author

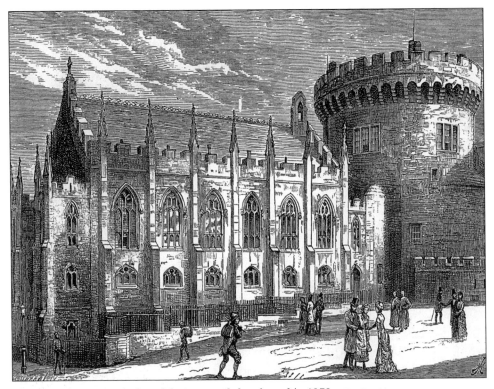

A view of the tower and chapel royal in 1878. The Graphic

Arms had been moved to the Castle in that year. There was a whole panoply of officers and honorary members entrusted with the safety of the jewels, including the Dublin Herald Frank Shackleton, who was the brother of the famous explorer. He became a suspect, because clearly the valuables had been stolen by someone with access to a key, and he lodged with Vicars at his home in Clonskeagh Road.

The main pieces of the collection were incredibly valuable. The star and badge had in them rubies, emeralds and Brazilian diamonds, and they were meant to be worn by the Lord Lieutenant of Ireland (in fact, a Viceroy) on ceremonial occasions. Estimates of their value today are around the figure of over a millions pounds. In 1907 they were valued at £40,000.

Sir Arthur Vicars was born in Leamington in 1864, the son of Sir Arthur Edward Vicars, Colonel in the 61st Regiment. He had been educated at Magdalen College, Oxford, and then in

1893 he was appointed as Ulster King of Arms. *The Times* wrote of him on his death, 'He was thoroughly versed in the sciences of heraldry and genealogy... He was a Fellow of the Royal Society of Antiquaries and a trustee of the National Library of Ireland.' Vicars had actually been the man who founded the Heraldic Museum at the Office of Arms. But all this counted for nothing after the disgrace and scandal of this daring and outrageous theft.

Vicars had in his possession the only two keys to the safe. One of the first lines of thought was that Shackleton had used or copied one of these. They had not actually been seen since 11 June, when Vicars had proudly shown them to a visitor, the librarian of the Duke of Northumberland. It was rare for anyone to open the safe but Vicars himself, and so for him to ask Stivey to open it, and to give him a key, on the day the theft was discovered, was a notable fact when the investigation began.

The police suspected Shackleton but on slender information, including the detail that a few days before the theft he had been heard to remark that one day the jewels might well be stolen. He was also in debt, and so had a motive.

It was a major scandal: the status of the Office of Arms was of the highest order; they had been established in 1552, and they administered the protocol and precedence at Dublin Castle. Vicars, as Ulster King of Arms was the Chief Herald of Ireland, Knight Attendant and

Frank Shackleton.
By kind permission of Mr Sean Murphy

registrar of the Order. In the records he was defined as 'the first and only permanent officer of the Lord Lieutenant's household'. A painting of Sir Arthur Vicars in his ceremonial dress is at the Castle, showing him in Elizabethan court garb, with doublet and ruff, and with the harp of Ireland prominent on the lower left side of his garments.

The police went into action. They issued a poster offering £1,000 reward for information leading to the retrieval of the jewels. They are described as having '150 white, pure diamonds issuing from the centre' and the badge was 'set in silver, with a shamrock of emeralds on a ruby cross surrounded by a sky blue enamelled circle – with their motto, *Quis Superabit* (who shall separate it).' The whole was 'surrounded by a circle of large single Brazilian stones, surmounted by a crowned harp in diamonds'.

There was to be a royal visit just four days after this discovery and that had, of course, been planned. There was to have been an investiture of a knight in St Patrick's Hall in the events of that visit, and of course that was something that caused a furore in London. The King, Edward VII, demanded that Vicars be sacked. There was a smear campaign against him, including accounts of orgies he was supposedly involved in, and the allegation that he was homosexual, which was then a criminal activity of course, and Oscar Wilde's trial was fresh in the public memory.

When it came to the establishment of a Viceregal Commission of Enquiry, after a period when there had been no success in the hunt for the villains, Vicars kept out of it. The Commission met in January 1908 and heard evidence from Shackleton. The due process of enquiry took place and in the end Vicars was totally at fault. It vindicated Shackleton and made it clear that Vicars was a disgrace to the office. The Commission was appointed by the Irish government and included Chester Jones, a London police magistrate and the Chief Commissioner of the Dublin Metropolitan Police. At the time, it was reported by the chairman that 'Sir Arthur Vicars had definitely declined to come forward to facilitate the Commission in any way. He recognised that the Commission had no power to control or to compel Sir Arthur Vicars to give evidence. The government considered that the enquiry should go forward...'

Vicars was dismissed and went to live in County Kerry where, on 14 April 1921, a party of IRA men shot him dead. *The Times* reported on his death that he had faced a mob of gunmen before, a year earlier, and had stood firm when they demanded the key to his strongroom. On that occasion they had left, but the second attack was more desperate and determined. He was taken from his bed in his dressing gown and murdered outside his house. A label was placed around his neck with the words, 'Spy, Informers beware. I.R.A. never forgets.' His house was then set on fire.

One theory about this mystery is that Shackleton and a rogue called Captain Gorges were responsible, but this is only a conjecture put forward in an article in *The Gaelic American* by Bulmer Hobson of the IRB. Hobson wrote that he had information to suggest that in one of many drunken parties, Shackleton had taken a key from Vicars as he slept, then the jewels were stolen, and that both Shackleton and Gorges had huge debts which led them to that desperate measure. Hobson also claimed that Shackleton had been energetically grilled by officers of the Dublin Metropolitan Police but there had been no conclusive evidence and that the authorities were content to know that Shackleton had left the country and was out of their hair.

Another suspect is one Francis Goldney, who was discovered (after his death) to have robbed antiquities from a range of places, including from the City of Canterbury and from the possessions of the Duke of Bedford. Goldney had been made Athlone Pursuivant (second in order of precedence to the Ulster King of Arms) in February 1907, and according to the historian Sean Murphy, 'grounds for suspicion certainly exist... but no hard evidence has been found to connect him with the theft of the Irish crown jewels, nor do contemporaries appear to have suggested that he might have been involved'.

Vicars was shot dead, and also Shackleton's later life confirmed certain opinions of him: in 1913 he was convicted of fraud, and then on release he died in Chichester in 1941. He is on record of saying, while in gaol, that he knew more about the theft than he had previously said, but nothing came of that. The case remains a mystery. But there is one fascinating coda to the tale: in 1976, some papers from William Cosgrave's estate were read and there was the statement that, in a government file of 1926, 'the castle jewels are for sale and they can be got for £2,000 or £3,000'. There have also been rumours that the jewels are stashed away at Three Rock in the Dublin Mountains. Writer and Dublin historian Frank Hopkins even suggests that some tales insist that the jewels are beneath the ruins of the Vicars' house in Kerry.

CHAPTER **20**

An Orgy of Anarchy
1913

*'Language has lost its sense if there is not here
a direct incitement to murder.'*
ARNOLD WRIGHT

T here have been a number of hellish and widespread riots in the history of Dublin, but few can compare with those of the year 1913 and the intermittent troubles in the years just before. The man who has taken the blame is Jim Larkin, and a voluminous book published just the year after by Arnold Wright has the flavour of a toady writing to please his master, such is its condemnation of Larkin, a great man who stands in the tradition of the Chartists, the orators Hunt, Tillett and other courageous left-wing dissidents who wanted to stop the exploitation of the downtrodden workers.

In the first decades of the twentieth century, Dublin certainly had its fair share of what sociologists used to call the 'underclass'. The poverty was extreme and there were serious and widespread problems of public health. Dublin witnessed a pattern of employer-union conflict which had been seen decades before in the northern cotton towns and in the London docks just twenty years earlier. The workers were from slum areas and the statistics of deprivation are staggering: in 1910 a third of the city's population lived in what we would call slums today; the infant mortality rate was 142 per thousand births – as bad as the cholera epidemic of the 1830s in Liverpool. TB was a regular deathly visitant to family homes, and the tenement living conditions meant that there were too many people in very cramped conditions. In one category of housing, there were 1516 tenements occupied by 8295 families. A contemporary writer has a story to tell about this social context:

*A Roman Catholic clergyman, the Rev. P.J. Monahan, C.C.,
who gave evidence, mentioned an instance in which 107*

human beings occupied one tenement house, stating that there were only two water-closets in the entire building for both sexes. His figures were challenged later by the corporation officials, who represented that the inmates numbered not 107 but 95, and that there were three water-closets... But the position of the inmates is dreadful to contemplate.

In terms of the work done by people from these homes, trade unionism was entering a place where it had not existed before and where, from the point of view of the major employers, it was a concept they hated and despised. The Irish had experienced this before in a remarkable historical parallel – that of 1830s Manchester, where Irish immigrant families there for work in the factories lived in overcrowded cellars, mostly ill and diseased, while the rich mill owners lived across town in their villas.

Trade union activity shines a torch into these dark places created by class difference, greed and the relentless machine of commerce grinding on, pushing for profits, while it spits out its human fodder. Into this climate came Jim Larkin, a man dogged by controversy, too militant even for his own dockers' union in

Where Larkin began: Liverpool Docks. The author

Liverpool and later in Belfast, and he came with a credo that was meant to upset the apple-cart of the bosses: 'The principle I state and mean to stand on is that the entire ownership of Ireland, moral and material, up to the sun and down to the centre, is vested of right in the people of Ireland.'

Larkin was from Liverpool, but of Irish parentage; he described himself as 'a foreign adventurer from the slum recesses of some clog-wearing town'. He had travelled to South America and seen some of the world; then, around 1907 he was organising dockers in Liverpool and Glasgow, and building a reputation that made enemies. He had called a strike in Ireland – at Dundalk and Newry – and then was involved in the major strike in Belfast in 1908. People complained about him at the Dockers' Congress and he was too busy to worry about that. He was planning an Irish organisation of labour, and what happened in 1910 was to increase his status and popularity with the Dublin working class – he was sent to prison. The Dockers' Union claimed that he had misappropriated some funds and he was given a sentence of one year, the offence allegedly having been committed in Cork.

But what did all that matter when he came out and started work again? To most people he was a workers' champion and he was ready to take on the employers. In Dublin there was one commercial tycoon in particular whom he took on: William Martin Murphy from Cork. Not only had Murphy won control of several major national newspapers and some factories, he was

Heroic Larkin lives on: his statue in O'Connell Street. The author

chairman of the Dublin United Tramway Company, and he even owned Clery's department store. He had expanded his tramway enterprises into England, though with limited success. Basically, he was 'Mr Dublin' in terms of power in the market and with the establishment of employers, in spite of the fact that he was Catholic in a location dominated by the Protestant Ascendancy power-base.

Larkin and his union philosophies were on the move; the paper, *The Irish Worker*, was his main outlet for communication, founded in 1911. The organ confronted and attacked not only capitalism but imperialism and of course, the employers themselves. Some of the most telling elements in that paper were the satirical poems, as in these lines attacking 'scabs' in strike activity:

> *Who shuns the face of the open day,*
> *Who wanders out in the gloomy grey,*
> *Who gets his price and sneaks away?*
> *The scab.*

Murphy's workers had better wages than average in Dublin, but they put in more hours for that. Many worked seventeen hours a day and were compelled to do so, and the workplace regime was stern and uncompromising. It has been argued that he established an 'informer culture' in that context. Murphy was a man with many staunch principles, and he kept to them,, even refusing a knighthood and sticking to that resolve even when Edward VII visited Dublin in 1907 when the Lord Lieutenant had forgotten Murphy's stance on the knighthood and had to cancel the ceremony even while the king sat waiting with sword in hand. The man who became Larkin's enemy was defended by his supporters in such a way that there is a deep contradiction in him; one writer described him as a kind man: 'The very last attribute that you would associate with this striking personality is tyranny... Few Dublin employers have a higher reputation for kindliness.' There is the contradiction: for some he was a monster with an obsession with profits and productivity and to others he was a kind, humane manager.

But Larkin and his Irish Transport and General Workers Union, which he had founded in December 1908, when he had

The Alarm Clock of Labour.

The alarm clock of the Irish working class is again ringing in loud and strident tones, calling on every man, woman and child who earns his or her daily bread by the sweat of the brow to Organise. "Unity is Strength" must be our slogan in the future, and unity on the industrial field can only be achieved by organisation. If the working class of this land desire to rise out of the mire into which economic conditions have forced them during the past years, they must Organise. Organise by getting into your Union. Be a Unionman. A Unionman is a class soldier; a non-Unionman is a class traitor, and class-treachery is the lowest form of treachery. Don't be a class traitor; get into a Union. If your Union won't fight, then make it fight; but be in a Union and organise-**Organise**-**ORGANISE**.

The Alarm Clock of Labour. Courtesy of the National Library of Ireland

left the dockers, gathered a membership of 5000 in its first year of existence. Murphy and the employers took them on, refusing to acknowledge their existence: on 15 August 1913, Murphy sacked first of all forty men whom he thought had joined, and then a week later, he sacked 300 more.

That was the trigger for trouble. Larkin had formed the notion of syndicalism – sympathetic strikes, so the domino-effect would happen; in Dublin it started with the tramway workers going on strike; drivers and conductors walked away from the trams, and there was chaos – notably because it was timed to disrupt the events at the Dublin Horse Show. Murphy responded by demanding that all employees signed a pledge not to belong to a union.

The strike accelerated, and the use of strong pickets and intimidation was sanctioned by Larkin; there was a workers' militia with James Connolly (who was to be shot in the yard of

11

Edited by Jim Larkin.

Vol. 2. No. 8.   SATURDAY, MARCH 14, 1925.   PRICE TWOPENCE.

JOHNSONIAN FUDGE

It is not for nothing that the imperialist Johnson, T.D., has declared that he is "not a Bolshevik." Likewise, it is not for nothing he has omitted to state (in recent years) that he is an imperialist.

The fact in each case is well known, though from time to time fresh evidence accrues to refresh our memory lest, perhaps, we forget.

Early this week the "Independent," through a "correspondent," started a hare and the leash-hounds of the Irish Labour Party, with an eye to election results, went in pursuit.

At a time when the Parliamentary system of Government is meeting with criticism from all sides, it is instructive and amusing to find it championed by the "Labour" group in Lower Abbey Street. It is instructive, because the defence lays bare the attitude of mind of the Johnsonian Party, and amusing because of the ill-concealed fear that something else should be found to take its place.

Several of the great European powers have had, within the last few years, the experience of "unstable Government." In most cases it was due to the multiplicity of political parties, none of them strong enough to rule separately, but in combination sufficiently powerful to obstruct the processes of Government by whatever party should accept office. Italy and Germany are cases in point. In the former, 'a way out was sought in a ~~Dictatorship~~, but Mussolini, like other men whose policy had no roots in the people, failed, and the results are daily becoming more evident.

The inadequacy of Parliament to meet the case of an electorate divided ~~into factions, through enough~~ ...

THE STIFLED VOICE OF THE WORKING CLASS

The election debauch is over, and now let us, who, regardless of the results, must still remain the bottom dogs, get together and try, in some definite manner, to realise our position, and by laying bare each political party, show the inability of these vote-catchers to express the desires of the working class.

We have first the Cumann na nGaedheal Party—the Government Party. The leaders of this Party have held the powers of Government for some years now, and during those years they have deliberately and unscrupulously carried out the programme laid down by the capitalist class of this country. This Government has beaten down wages, lengthened hours, used armed force in strikes, reduced Old Age Pensions, and used the whole force of the State to crush the power of Labour in the country. They hold out no promises to our class; they appeal solely to the monied, selfish, reactionary section of the people. They are openly an anti-Labour Party.

The Sinn Fein Party is the next requiring examination. This Party candidly admits its inability to lighten the burden of our class in any small way until such times as they obtain Governmental power. Though many of their leaders are sympathetic to our class, yet they tell us we must wait till their particular system of Government is established—but in the meantime we must live, have bread to eat, houses to live in, and means to educate our children—and our problem is how to get these necessities. In the elections now past the most class-conscious workers voted for this Party's candidates, because each vote for this Party was a blow against our immediate enemies—the Government, who are our present and heaviest oppressors.

The Sinn Fein Party, like their political opponents, hold out no hope for us. Let us proceed further.

We have next the Farmers' Party. This Party is formed exclusively of ~~farmers—mostly big land-owners. They are fighting solely for their own benefit~~—they want their interests fostered by the State. Our interests and their interests are opposed. We are the wage-slaves—the agricultural labourers—and they are the employers—the farmers. We and they are economic enemies. They want smaller wages; we must have bigger wages if we are to live other than as beasts. This Party does not ask for our votes; they rely on their fellow land-owners for political power.

might not occur to him as comparable with the aspect of a herd of lowly cattle travelling homeward in a cloud of dust. Yet, in Great Britain there is an awakening, and before many years, the process of enlightenment may have advanced to the point where "unstable Government" shall be a reality. It may be that the intermediate stage of development of class-consciousness, represented by a multiplicity of political parties in Parliament, may be avoided and that the workers of Great Britain will pass directly from the Parliamentary system to control by workshop, factory and field—but this is speculative. The actual development will depend on the nature of working-class leadership, and the effectiveness, or otherwise, of the policy of sabotage which will undoubtedly be followed by the reactionary Labour parties. In Ireland, re-action is personified in the members of the Irish Labour Party, and their attitude as to the governance of the people is expressed in the letters of two of their number published in an "Independent" of the present week, Messrs. Johnson, T.D., and O'Connell, T.D., in pursuit of the "Independent," have opened their minds on the subject as follows:—

Mr. Johnson:—" Your correspondent . . . . is too tired to think out the implications of his own contentious. He is clearly tired of Parliamentary institutions; he wants a Dáil consisting of one Party only, a Government, but no opposition . . . ."

We can imagine Mr. Johnson's horror of a Dáil representative of Labour only—a Worker's Republic. Let us say—and his agony of soul at the absence of the Business fraternity, the Farmers' Party and the blessed Independent Party. If Mr. Johnson were not "too tired to think out the

From The Irish Worker.   Courtesy of the National Library of Ireland

Kilmainham Gaol by the British in 1916) and Jack White also involved in command. Jack White (ex British officer) styled his men the Irish Citizen Army. There was soon violence in the streets and confrontation with the law. In August 1913, two workers died and there were several more injuries in Sackville Street (now O'Connell Street where Larkin's statue stands) and there was a baton charge by the police.

The Sackville Street riot happened largely because Larkin attended. He boldly arrived to speak outside the *Imperial Hotel*, owned by Murphy, and Larkin was arrested. The meeting had been banned by the Lord Mayor but that counted for nothing. Larkin had been bailed but was then pursued for re-arrest. There was a massive police presence that Sunday 31 August, and constables had been instructed to let people pass freely along the street but that no 'assemblage of persons' was to be allowed. There were 274 constables, 23 sergeants and 9 inspectors present.

After half-past twelve, the crowd began to gather; the main assembly was by the General Post Office and Larkin, appearing at the *Imperial Hotel*, was of course greeted enthusiastically. But the trigger for real trouble happened when it was seen that police were going into the hotel, clearly intending to arrest Larkin. People in the crowd threw objects at police and a large plate glass window was thrown. There was then a baton charge. The police report on the worst phase of the conflict was evidence of disgraceful conduct, as typified by this:

> *In one regrettable instance, that of Mr O'Donnell, a respectable gentleman carrying on business in Lower Sackville Street received very severe injuries at the hands of the police. There were thirteen police injured during the course of this riot...*

There was a hearing about the riot at which questions were asked by Handel Booth MP and he cross-examined the various police superintendents present. Even at this meeting there was aggression, as Booth accused one officer of suppressing evidence.

Trouble did not end in Sackville Street that day, yet another Irish 'Bloody Sunday': in the Cornmarket and Thomas Street there was more rioting. This started around five o'clock that same day when mobs of hundreds of people attacked tramcars

Aungier Street – scene of desperate fighting during the lock-out. The author

on the College Green to Inchicore route. Police escorts had to be provided. Stones and bottles were thrown and a constable was badly injured. A group of police made arrests and took the offenders to Chancery Lane bridewell, over the Liffey, so they had a fairly long walk, and then had to return to the trouble spot. In Meath Street a sergeant and eighteen constables were viciously attacked by a large and violent group of about 200 people who threw bricks and bottles at them. In Cornmarket there were over 600 people rioting and there was another baton charge. There were, according to some accounts, organised attacks on police. As one writer noted, just a year after these riots, 'Eleven policemen were injured – some of them very seriously – they behaved with courage and forbearance, and there was no use of unnecessary force in dealing with the rioters.' That was a statement that not all involved would agree with.

There were further trouble spots across the city, and trams

The Shelbourne Hotel. The author

were the main targets. In Aungier Street police reinforcements were sent in, and a sergeant ordered batons drawn. Then this small group of officers was attacked by a massive crowd coming out from Longford Street. In that riot, one tram conductor was very severely hurt and was in hospital for two weeks afterwards.

One of the worst incidents was in Redmond's Hill and Wexford Street where, after making arrests, a party of police returned to the fray and found themselves assailed by hundreds of people with stones and bricks; the sergeant shouted for the crowd not to stone them. He was an experienced officer and that was a very brave thing to do, but unfortunately it had no effect. He and his men were forced to run and were stoned all the way to Stephen's Green.

After the disturbances, it was recorded that 656 people were arrested. Almost 200 of these had previous convictions. There was a conference held at the *Shelbourne Hotel* on 6 December and employers issued a statement which essentially was summed up by Arthur Henderson: 'When the present dispute is over the employers undertake to confer with the representatives of the workers with a view to framing a scheme or schemes for the prevention or settlement of future disputes.' But the workers wanted all men reinstated of course. Nothing was worked out to everyone's satisfaction.

The lock-out following this continued until attempts at sympathetic strikes across the Irish Sea failed and in 1914 Larkin went to America. But there had been an achievement: union action had been seen to be effective and very damaging; some firms were bankrupt, and the ITGWU had to be redeveloped – this time by William O'Brien. As for Martin Murphy, he has the dubious distinction of figuring negatively in one of the poems written by W B Yeats at the time, in which we have these lines about him: 'Your enemy, an old foul mouth had set the pack upon him.'

CHAPTER 21

Mountjoy Tales
1900–1960

*'If our lot had not been so small in this world we might
not occupy a place in a prison but be members of society...'*
THOMAS D'ARCY

Mountjoy Prison, on the North Circular Road, opened its doors to prisoners on 27 March 1850. It had been designed, as so many gaols in England had been, on the Pentonville model, with a central tower and radial wings, surrounded by a *cordon sanitaire* and the outer walls and gate.

In the nineteenth century, its story was the same as so many others – a place for men, women and children, and a place alternately influenced by philosophies of retribution,

*The destiny of an earlier Mountjoy prisoner: William Smith O'Brien's house
in Port Arthur.* The author

punishment and rehabilitation. The regime of a prison is military and the men who ran them in the years from the beginnings to recent times were often men with military backgrounds. The crimes were the usual ones associated with poverty and dire straits – larceny, robbery, theft, assault, fraud and so on. The crimes against the person were punished with the lash for many years and physical punishment of various kinds was the order of the day in the Victorian period.

By the twentieth century, there were all kinds of different prisoners, many not related to the average felon, such as political prisoners with good educations, such as Francis Sheehy-Skeffington, the subject of the next chapter, who was given a six-months sentence in 1915 for making an anti-war speech. Of course, after the Easter Rising of 1916 and the Defence of the Realm Act played its part in the general suppression. Mountjoy was mainly functioning as a 'local' or dispersal prison, with regard to the political prisoners, who were mostly sent to gaols in England, such as de Valera's trip to HMP Lincoln. But many of the twentieth century Mountjoy tales are linked to crimes of activists and militants for various causes, as well as of career criminals and small-time crooks.

One of the most dramatic and controversial sagas from inside its walls is that of the women of the Irish Women's Franchise League. In 1912, the suffragist paper, *The Irish Citizen*, threatened a hunger strike in Mountjoy; the focus for this was Mrs Mary Leigh. She and some others had been given long sentences for trying to burn the Theatre Royal on the night of Herbert Asquith's visit, and the *Irish Citizen* made clear its position on that act and its significance:

> *The savage sentences inflicted on the convicted prisoners, cannot, of course, be allowed to stand. The judge himself was sufficiently ashamed of them to express the hope that they would speedily be revised by the proper authority... The Irish public must not fall behind the disagreeing jurymen in the appreciation of the political motive of Mrs. Leigh and her comrades. They must be accorded the full rights of political prisoners.*

A hunger strike was planned. There was fury that Mrs Leigh

had a term of five years to serve. The five years were of penal servitude as well; there was no stretch of knitting and sewing to be considered. By 3 September the force-feeding had begun; on that date it was reported that Mrs Leigh was 'in a state of collapse'. A supporter, Mrs Grace Roe of Dublin, went to speak to the Lord Lieutenant about the matter. She was told that it was policy from England that was the cause: Asquith and Lloyd George wanted it done, and even Lord Aberdeen could not persuade them otherwise. The two women in question, Leigh and Miss Evans, were reported on by *The Times* and the news was not good in the autumn of 1912, the correspondent from Dublin writing that he had no reason to believe 'that Sir James Dougherty gave Miss Roe ... absolutely no hope of the early release of the prisoners...'

By October, though, Leigh was released on compassionate grounds, and was facing trial for yet another offence. She had thrown a hatchet at John Redmond, a Home Rule supporter of Asquith, on that same occasion of Asquith's visit. Mr Justice Kenny announced that there would be a full investigation with regard to that second charge against her.

In December, the Cat and Mouse Act began to take effect on Leigh and Evans. In lawyer speak, they had 'failed to comply with the terms of their licence on release from Mountjoy'. They had not reported to police by the time set, and so they were to be returned to gaol but were bailed pending an appeal to the King's Bench with the objection that they were not in fact obliged to report while on their licence.

In 1924 there were scenes of a very different kind when a police van was ambushed by armed men while taking prisoners to Mountjoy. The attack took place on Goldsmith Street near the prison. There were sixteen prisoners in the van, which was horse-drawn, and there were gangs of young men around the street corners, waiting for what was in effect a battle to commence. Around one-thirty on 13 April that year, the van driver saw that there was trouble and tried to take a short cut, going through Goldsmith Street, but there was a blockade across the road – a large green van. There was also a line of men on the street, all with revolvers. The driver bravely whipped up his horses and galloped by the only gap there was, making it to the prison. The gunmen fired at the van but did not halt its progress. By that time the escort arrived – two detectives – and there was a gun fight in the street. Amazingly, no-one was shot, and although there were bullet holes in the van, none had hit anyone.

Two of the prisoners in the van had been charged with attempted murder, and one of the men was a former captain in the Free State army: John Wilson. The charge against him was an attempt to shoot dead a police officer, Richard O'Connell, while the officer was trying to arrest him by Stephen's Green.

Another disturbance outside the gaol involved Dominick Behan the author, after he and four other men had assaulted police officers outside Mountjoy. Behan, a great song-writer and writer, was the nephew of Peadar Kearney, the man who wrote *The Soldier's Song*. He had already been in gaol, the year before, for leading a civil disobedience campaign against the government's alleged incompetence in matters of economics. His republican pedigree also included the place his father had in the infamous hit-men of Michael Collins, the 'Twelve Apostles'.

Far less noble and momentous was this particular affray, in which Behan and his pals only succeeded in assaulting Constable John Purtell. But one thing was notable about the trial – it was closed to the public and press, and the defence counsel, Lehane, protested at that. So yet again, in whatever he did, Behan made a furore and got into the papers. His play, *Posterity be Damned*, was produced at the Gaiety thirteen years after this incident, and following that, he wrote for television in later life and wrote some of the most influential songs of the period, including *The Patriot Game* and *Famine Song*.

Of all the twentieth century Mountjoy tales, one of the darkest has to be the issue of the hangman. It had always been the practice for English hangmen to cross over to Ireland to conduct executions, but in 1945 a man with the assumed name of 'Thomas Johnston' was appointed the Irish hangman. But he had had little training, and in 1946 when Joseph McManus was sentenced to death for a murder in Meath, Johnston was to be the man responsible for the judicial hanging. He asked permission to be assistant, as he did not feel confident to do the job. The expert Albert Pierrepoint came over to take the lead. Pierrepoint had given Johnston some basic training at Strangeways, but in the case of McManus, it became obvious that Johnston could not cope and Pierrepoint checked and handled every stage of the process; the hanging went smoothly in the end. When Pierrepoint and Johnston parted and went their separate ways, Johnston did not hint that he had had enough of the job, but that was the case. Ireland still did not have a hangman, and left it to the British after that.

Pierrepoint was back in Mountjoy in 1945 to hang Canadian, James Lehman, who had been living in Leinster Road, Rathmines. He was a family man, with a wife and two children. Lehman was a womaniser and had started a relationship with a local nurse when he realised that telling lies was useful; he told the nurse that he was not actually married to his wife, Margaret. But from the lie the fantasy extended into desperation and he planned his wife's death. Lehman ran a retail coffee firm and so he had a seemingly legitimate reason to buy cyanide from a Leinster Road chemist, saying it was needed for doing a chemical test in the bottling process.

On 19 March 1944, he put the cyanide into some rum his wife was drinking. She was in agony, her whole skin turning into

Aerial view of Mountjoy Prison in 1949. Irish Times

a deep purple hue as she was rushed to hospital. She did not even reach the end of that journey, dying in the ambulance. Lehman, conman and dangerous dreamer that he was, was a slippery customer and took a while to track down, but he was caught and became a customer for Mr Pierrepoint. This time everything went smoothly.

We have a dramatic depiction of Pierrepoint in Brendan Behan's play *The Quare Fellow*. Behan did a stretch in Mountjoy and he must have known the atmosphere in the place before an execution. He has his hangman character sing Irish songs and talk about his pub at home in Manchester. Behan captures the prison atmosphere with sensitivity and power when he had a character sing a song interspersed with the hang man calculating the length of drop. The hangman says, 'I've never wanted for friends. Do you know why? Because I'd go a hundred miles to do a man a good turn. I've always tried to do my duty.'

There were German spies held at Mountjoy as well, and the remarkable tale of Hans Schuetz, who escaped from Mountjoy, provides us with an unbelievable error by the governor of the time. Prison work and the basic security measures enforced in a prison regime involves a keen sensitivity to any matter pertaining to clothes and dress, as in the instances of such things as prison drama productions where wigs and disguise might be worn. For obvious reasons, sanction for such things would have to be very carefully considered and then, should clothing be granted, the vigilance needed to check for misuse would be very acute. But the governor in 1942 allowed the prisoner the purchase of a set of women's clothes supposedly to take home to his sister.

Schuetz had been parachuted into Wexford and was soon captured and given a seven-year stretch. But in 1942 he had managed to acquire a saw and he sawed through bars, made it to the outer wall along with a Dutch prisoner called Van Loon. They escaped and the German was housed with Cathal Bruha's widow Caitlin. But he was recaptured there and then taken to Arbour Hill Gaol. Most of the German spies were returned to their homeland in 1947.

CHAPTER 22

War Crime by a Madman
1916

'It was clearly my duty to have the three ring-leaders shot…'
CAPTAIN BOWEN-COLTHURST

This is the only story in this book that relates in any way to a political confrontation, but it is a tale to freeze the blood. Shortly after the Easter Rising on 24 April 1916, Portobello Barracks was a place where all kinds of military personnel were arriving to gather and sort out where they should be and what they should be doing. One of these was Captain J C Bowen-Colthurst of the Irish Rifles. His decision to take a raiding-party out into the streets led to what we can only call mass murder; it had nothing to do with the suppression of a perceived rebellion and was entirely unrelated to any definable action by troops of Britain.

The time was right in the midst of the action by the Irish Citizen Army and the Volunteers to prise the city from the British. It had been a time of high drama indeed, with the usual chaos and confusion of urban warfare: snipers and random patrols likely to turn up anywhere and threats to soldiers existing as they might do in a guerrilla combat. But none of this was an excuse for what Bowen-Colthurst was to do that day.

Out went the raiding party, and they came across Francis Sheehy-Skeffington, Thomas Dickson and Patrick MacIntyre. Sheehy-Skeffington was a pacifist and had no connection with the uprising that Easter. The raiding party consisted of a junior officer and forty men – a formidable force to make random arrests. Bowen-Colthurst had the idea to raid a tobacconist's shop owned by Alderman James Kelly, maybe confusing the name with that of Tom Kelly, and he thought it would be wise to have a hostage – Sheehy-Skeffington – to take along. The group had only got as far as a little way outside the barracks when they came across a young man called Coade who was going home from church, and there was the first atrocity of the raid – the crazed officer gave orders for the soldiers to hit him, and one soldier smashed the boy's jaw with his rifle. Then Bowen-Colthurst shot the boy as he lay on the ground; Coade was just seventeen years old.

The prisoners had no connection at all with Sinn Fein or the ICA. But back at the barracks the murderous officer was in that mad frame of mind in which 'martial law' could be a situation in which anything could be done, however savage, in the name of right and justice. He had found some papers in Kelly's shop and he looked at these as his prisoners awaited their fate. He then decided that he wanted the captives out in the yard and then he said, 'I am taking these prisoners out and I am going to shoot them as I think that is the right thing to do.'

'Martial law' simply means that an authority is giving warning that the military powers will take unusual measures to make sure that order is maintained in the community – no more than that. But this officer, who later claimed that he thought his prisoners to be desperate men and 'leaders of the rebels' interpreted the notion of martial law as carte blanche to indulge in murder and atrocity. He had in fact shot two loyalists and a writer. Sheehy-Skeffington was born in Baileborough, Co Cavan and had been educated at University College Dublin, where he was a friend of James Joyce. He married the feminist Hannah Sheehy and had kept her name to show his sympathy with the cause of equality. So this man was a pacifist, intellectual and social campaigner. He had founded a journal, the *Irish Citizen* and supported the socialist and Labour parties. He actually disapproved of the rising, and yet here he was, an innocent man caught up in the anarchy of that 'Poets' Rising'.

The deranged officer had done something totally outrageous, and the commander of the barracks, Francis Fletcher Vane, was away from his base at the time. When the murderer did respond to demands for some kind of explanation, he said that he had placed the men in the yard even though he now said that the yard was a place from which they could have escaped. That was no kind of reason, and the second one, that he was 'unstrung' mentally was much nearer the truth. The first response to the offence was, from Major Rosborough, to put Bowen-Colthurst on non-combative duties, 'only to be employed on the defences of Portobello barracks, and not outside'.

SINN FEIN REBELLION

D.B.C. SACKVILLE STREET, DUBLIN.   BEFORE AND AFTER

Postcard of the 1916 Rising. Author's collection

Hanna, the wife of Francis Sheehy-Skeffington, came to the barracks to find out some information, and Bowen-Colthurst had them thrown out. One of the most disgusting details of this wholly intolerable display of crazed killing was that it was only when young Coade's father saw the corpse of the missing pacifist lying by the side of his son that the facts were known.

It was only down to the determined actions of Francis Fletcher Vane that any justice took place in this case; he had returned to army service after a break (following time in the Boer War). He was sent to Ireland with the rank of major, and he took command of the Portobello barracks, with around 300 men under his command. He had been away supervising observation posts while this atrocity was done, and when he returned he immediately did what should have been done before – he confined the offender to barracks and moved to obtain a military court-martial.

This happened, under the guidance of Lord Reading, but it only happened after Vane had pressed for it, including a trip to England for a private meeting with Lord Kitchener, who responded with a command for a trial. Reading, the Lord Chief Justice, presided as it was conducted in camera; Bowen-Colthurst was found guilty but insane. This was only the beginning for Fletcher Vane, and indeed for Hanna Sheehy-Skeffington. The injustice was extreme and demanded further action, including compensation. To make matters worse, the offender was released from Broadmoor after just one year of incarceration. When an offer of compensation came to Hanna, she refused it.

Fletcher Vane and Hanna campaigned for the truth to come out, and eventually even Theodore Roosevelt responded to the implications of the incident, writing to Vane and saying, 'I write to you

Skeffington outrage reported abroad, New York Times, *1917.*

New York Times

upon the assurance of Mrs Skeffington that you are willing to give the facts. I have no personal interest in the matter. But I have unhesitatingly condemned the Germans for the atrocities they have committed; I have always announced that I would just as strongly condemn atrocities of like character committed by the allies; I do not feel at liberty to refuse Mrs Skeffington's request that I satisfy myself as to the truth of her statement.'

Fletcher Vane repeatedly tried to write about the incident, and even tried to publish a book about the Easter Rising; he came up against censorship and suppression, with his proof copies being taken from him. It was not until 1930 that his book finally appeared: *Agin the Government*, and the text contained all his reflections on the Bowen-Colthurst affair. He is surely one of the most admirable Dubliners in history, and yet he is not widely known nor suitably honoured. He was born in 1861 in

Portobello: the area in peace time, from an 1890 directory. Author's collection

Great George's Street, and surely there is a case for a commemorative plaque to be placed there. After all, he was the man who consistently aroused indignation in the face of the affair; John Dillon, MP made sure that the House of Commons knew about it too, but all the rhetoric of indignation falls into second place by the side of a letter written to the *Down Recorder* by Francis Sheehy-Skeffington's father, in which he wrote, amongst other things, 'In reference to the death of my beloved son, I wish to impress that he was never a Sinn Feiner nor a Volunteer. He was in no way connected with any physical force body; on the contrary, he was totally opposed to such means.' His son had even been busy putting up notices opposing the despicable looting of shops during the rising. The only possible reference that the deranged officer could have seen in the papers he took from Hanna's home might have been some detail about his former status as chairman of the ICA when it was part of James Larkin's movement for labour reforms. But Francis had resigned from that position in 1914. Such a fine point would have escaped the officer, bent on a killing that night, to satisfy some deeply twisted hatred.

CHAPTER 23

Murder and Mayhem in Malahide
1926
'I am the victim of bribery and perjury.'
HENRY MCCABE

I t was April Fool's Day in 1926 when *The Times* reported that gardener Henry McCabe was reported to have been passing an old country house called La Mancha when he saw that it was on fire. The report was that, 'he ran into the grounds, to find that the doors were locked, and having failed to arouse the inhabitants, he rushed to the Malahide Police Station, where he gave the alarm'. He was certainly trying to fool somebody, and for a while he did so. A mystery emerged from that situation – a case of multiple deaths and a blaze in a beautiful old house. Six dead bodies were found inside when the Dublin Fire Brigade arrived and managed to get inside through a basement window.

The firemen struggled to find a way in, because the doors were all barred and bolted. But as they fought their way through all the rooms, they found first of all James Clarke dead on the kitchen floor. He was a servant of the family who owned the property, the McDonnells. As the search went on, the men next came across Peter McDonnell, and he was naked on the sitting-room floor; then upstairs his two sisters, Annie and Alice, were found dead, along with their servant, Mary Magowan. The women's bodies had been badly burned. Finally, the other brother, Joseph, was found dead also. What was discovered and told to the press early on was that there had been a violent attack and that the first two bodies found had been killed before the fire was started.

It was soon ascertained that the fire was actually started by someone; an empty tin of petrol was found, and it was noticed that fires had been started in three rooms downstairs. The top floor had also been burnt and totally ruined. It took several hours to put out the flames and after that more information

DUBLIN MANSION FIRE.

SIX DEAD BODIES FOUND.

BELIEVED MURDER AND ARSON.

(FROM OUR OWN CORRESPONDENT.)

DUBLIN, MARCH 31.

Six dead bodies were found in a burning house at Malahide, Co. Dublin, this morning in mysterious circumstances which suggest murder and arson.

At about half-past 8 a gardener named Henry Maccabe, of Parnell Cottages, Malahide, was passing an old country house. La Mancha, which stands in its

The arson as reported in The Times. The Times

came to light which gave the police the beginnings of a narrative of those events that they would have to put together – that was the discovery of a bloodstained poker.

The usual enquiries were made into the McDonnells as the search began for possible enemies, motives and reasons for any antipathy in the area towards the family from Ballygar, Roscommon. The slaughtered were all middle-aged, and had lived in Malahide for six years. They were well-liked and there were no known enemies or feuds that might have been linked to that horrendous attack and mass murder. The servant who was killed first was destined to be a part of the slaughter – he had just returned from holiday and came home very late – apparently just a little time before the arsonist and killer.

It took only ten days to find a suspect and, as usual in such cases, the person who reported the deed was the main suspect. There was a coroner's court led by Thomas Early, and that had to be adjourned until post-mortems could be done. Before the suspect was arrested, there had been some days of frustration for the police, as only after the pathology was complete was there any fragment of a chance that there might be a lead. But then a fuller story emerged and the arrest of Henry McCabe was announced. He was detained in the Malahide Police Station. The series of events was then put together, starting with a call at the house by a rate-collector a day before the fire led to the fact that at that time the house had been locked and was silent. McCabe was charged with six counts of murder before the Police Commissioner, Mr McMahon, and he was soon on remand in Mountjoy Prison.

After details had been given on the post-mortem reports by Francis Fogarty and Peter O'Toole of the State Laboratory, McCabe stood in Kilmainham District Court and there it was learned that McCabe had allegedly used arsenic, as that poison had been found in all six bodies.

At the trial at the Central Criminal Court the press and public had six days of reports and statements on this very nasty case; statements had been taken from eighty people and over the trial period there were sixty-three witnesses in court. McCabe's reign of terror at La Mancha had included brutal physical attacks on his victims and then the administering of arsenic. The court report made the point that 'all the bodies bore dreadful wounds'. The judge, Mr Justice O'Byrne, said in his summing up that there had been no-one from the family seen by anyone at all except the man in the dock; he stated that McCabe 'was the only person who had the opportunity to commit the crime'.

The horrible facts were plain and powerful: the use of a can of paraffin and a candlestick had been ascertained, and all three men had died from fractured skulls quite clearly done by the impact of a blunt instrument. What emerged was that McCabe had been so stupid that he had some of his victims' clothing at his house. He had set out to rob the family, but had been violent from the beginning, hitting Clarke with a spanner from behind as he sat down to milk a cow. After that he had put small quantities of arsenic into the food of the victims remaining alive and forced them to their beds before starting the fires. His other fires were a vain effort to cover up all the murderous activity.

It took the jury fifty minutes to decide on a verdict of guilty, and all McCabe said before sentence was passed was 'All I have to say is God forgive them. I am the victim of bribery and perjury.' The death sentence was given, and McCabe had a date with the hangman on 9 December 1926. There was a desperate appeal, and this was heard on 23 November when he had applied for legal aid and a transcript of the trial. His application for appeal was granted but it came to nothing.

Thomas Pierrepoint hanged Henry McCabe, forty-eight-years-old, on 9 December 1926. The death was unremarkable for Pierrepoint, with no obstacles and stresses above the usual. Dubliners were more than happy to see this killer exit the world and leave them feeling a little safer. The callous murderer would never have expected to figure in a major work of literature by one of the great twentieth century Irish writers, but in fact the murderous gardener's exploits were fictionalised by Samuel Beckett in his book *More Pricks Than Kicks* eight years after the hanging (1934).

CHAPTER 24

Blood Everywhere
1936

'I do not feel like saying anything at the moment.'
EDWARD BALL, ON BEING ARRESTED.

Shankill, a small village in 1936, close to the sea and to Bray, has had few murders in its chronicles, but the killing of Vera Ball in February of that year was a very rare event in murder – it was a case of matricide. It all started when a man delivering newspapers saw an Austin car stuck in a street in a place where vehicles would not normally be found. When he went to inspect he had a terrible shock – the interior was covered in blood and on the back seat there was a towel soaked in blood.

The man went to the police and when the Garda came to investigate they found blood below the car as well, and on a tyre. They soon found whose car this was, because of the papers inside. That led them to the home of Mrs Vera Ball in St Helen's Road, Booterstown. What happened then was to be the beginning of a very straightforward track to the solution of the mystery, because a maid in the house said that Edward, one of Vera's two sons, had recently come to live with them from Dublin, as he was hard up. But more importantly, she said quite plainly that mother and son did not get on well at all; in fact Edward was a drifter, a man who dreamed of an acting career but was basically unsound and very difficult.

When the detectives returned they found Edward Ball at home; he had assembled a scenario in his head and the thespian in him started to fabricate a tale, saying that he had seen his mother drive away in her car the day before. He was twenty, and his mother had not been very happy about having him back to live with her, but he told police that she had done so out of a sense of duty – after all, he was not twenty-one yet. He mentioned only a very minor incident (the smashing of a cup) when asked if he had fought with his mother recently. He was very cool at this

SON CHARGED WITH KILLING MOTHER

ACCUSED MAN'S STORY OF SUICIDE

In the Dublin District Court yesterday EDWARD PRESTON BALL, of 19, Booterstown, Co. Dublin, appeared on remand on the charge of having murdered his mother, Mrs. Lavena Ball, on February 17.

Mrs. Ball's abandoned motor-car was found in a lane at Shankill, Co. Dublin, on that date, and the supposition was that she had been killed and that her body had been thrown into the sea. Elaborate searches and dragging operations however, failed to reveal any trace of the body. Shortly afterwards her son was injured by a fall from a window of her house, and was charged with the murder in Richmond Hospital, Dublin, whence he was removed to Mountjoy Prison last Monday. His neck and wrist were still in bandages when he appeared in Court yesterday.

How The Times *reported the Ball case.* The Times

meeting, dealing with a question about the blood-soaked towel calmly, saying only that maybe there had been some kind of accident and a window had had to be forced open.

But the questioning intensified; there was so much material detail in the house – men's mud-stained shoes, a package of bloodstained linen in paper, and then the fact of the locked bedroom where his mother slept. Ball said that she always locked the room if she left the house. The door of that room was forced open, and from the scene the police saw there, some developments were significant. The details of the room were very significant: an electric fire was burning and there was a clear reason for that, because there was a patch of wet on a carpet. The two really telling details in the bedroom were that a rug was missing, and then the first fact to create definite suspicion in the minds of the detectives, the clothes in the wardrobe were the ones Edward Ball had told them his mother had been wearing when he last saw her.

It was in Ball's interests to try to fabricate a scenario which would suggest a possible case of suicide. By being sure that she would not try to take her life, he had planted a suggestion. Then, no doubt using his acting talents, he said that 'She's a great fighter, with all her troubles.' But the investigation intensified, with Ball in centre stage; there were lots of minor details about his actions over the previous few days that led to suspicion, such as cuts on his arms and a deep cut on a thumb. He had also been seen leaving the house carrying a suitcase. But there was indeed blood everywhere when it came to his own clothes, and police checks on him had led to the discovery that he had been to a local chemist to try to get stain-removing chemical substances. The following searches for clues and hunt for bloodstains, now that the line of thought was clear - that Mrs Ball had been killed at home – led to a list of detected stains, on stairs, walls, bed, carpets, clothes and bed linen. The pressure was on the young man, and arguably a letter found containing harsh words to him from his mother seemed to confirm the hidden nature of the relationship. She had written: 'I want you to understand that if you stay here tonight I am going to Mrs Allen. You did the usual dirty trick. Coming in at 12 o'clock last night; it has upset me. I am three hours late for my work, but what can I expect?'

It was not long before Ball realised that he had to find an explanation for the blood and he returned to the suicide tale, saying he had come home and found her body in bed, her throat cut. His vain argument for all this was that he had been concerned at her good name, as suicide was of course a crime as well as a sin at that time. But things came to a head when Ball, watched by a constable, went upstairs and then tried to take his own life. Launching himself out of a window two storeys high. He survived, though very severely injured. Suicide notes were found on him, including the statement: 'The events of the last two days have been unbearable and I claim the right to take my own life.'

He was charged with murder. When arrested by Super-intendent Dunleavy, Ball said, 'I do not feel like saying anything at the moment.' He was in hospital at Richmond for the court; George Cussen, senior District Justice, stood at the head of the bed, and the registrar sat by a small table. Justice Cussen granted a remand of a week and he asked for a full medical report on Ball. The prisoner had a broken arm and also his neck was fractured, so he could not be mobbed for some time.

By 26 March the trial at the Dublin District Court could proceed, and by that time Ball had been mobbed to Mountjoy Prison. The defence stated Balls case as one of his having acted desperately after the alleged suicide of his mother; he was sticking to the story he had told at home when faced with the bloodied clothes and furniture. His counsel said that Ball had been asked by his mother to protect her if ever she did 'anything stupid' and so when he found her body, he took it by car to Shankill and then dumped it in the sea.

On the other hand, prosecution said that the relations between mother and son during some months of the previous year had been 'extremely unhappy and of a distressing nature'.

Mr Justice Hanna, presiding, heard evidence that Mrs Ball used to scream at her son and she was described as being 'highly strung'. To back up the suicide case, the father, Dr Ball, said that ever since their marriage in 1902 his wife had suicidal tendencies and that there had been suicides in her family history. Edward was following in that line of illness, said his father. It was going to be difficult to build a case of matricide. But there were four pints of blood on the carpet and even blood on an axe out in a garden shed. But there was no body found, so everything was theoretical at the first stage. But the strongest evidence against Ball was from a pathologist, Dr John McGrath, who said that the death was not suicide. A hatchet had been used on her head and hair; had she cut her throat while on the carpet, where the highest concentration of blood was found, there was no way she could have got herself back into bed.

Against the matricide theory was the solid defence position, supported by expert witnesses from the field of psychiatry, who stated that Ball was mentally abnormal. The diagnosis was that he had dementia praecox. This was seen at the time as something related not only to a mental illness but to a related condition of 'moral deficiency'. That explained his lack of emotion at his mother's death and also his extraordinary ability in carrying her out in the rug and then driving her out to Shankill to throw her into the sea.

The search for a body went on, and that entailed trying to

ascertain where her body would have gone with the knowledge of the tidal flows from that beach. Experts came in to help, and police threw two oil drums in the sea at Shankill: one came to the coast in Wales and the other in Wicklow. The puzzle was turning into a mystery, but at the core of it all was the issue of insanity.

Looking at the case today, what stands out in the circumstances we have is that there was a process of careful action by Ball, a steady elimination of evidence being the intention, but what he did fell far short of that. The stages he went through in trying to hide all the blood and the various pieces of material evidence suggest careful, intended decision, by a rational mind. The pathology makes it clear that suicide was very unlikely. On top of that, it does seem highly probable, bearing in mind the statements of the maids at the house about Mrs Ball's cruelty and harshness to her son, that it would be highly likely that we have a case of 'the worm turning' here.

The defence of insanity had always been problematical in the courts. The definite case in terms of the provision of some kind of legal touchstone was the 'McNaughten Rules', referring to the case of Daniel McNaughten who had tried to assassinate Robert Peel in 1843 and had only succeeded in killing his secretary. McNaughten was classified as insane and escaped the noose. Would the same apply to Edward Ball? This was all about proving that a killer at the time of taking a life was suffering from an abnormality of mind.

The jury in Ball's case had to consider this, and with no concept of 'diminished responsibility' (that came in 1957 with the Homicide Act). They found him guilty but insane. It was clear that he would have to be kept for life in a mental hospital for the criminally insane. Of course, there was no body available, so that added another dimension of confusion. Add to that the aspects of sympathy for the young man – his attempted suicide and his general nature as a suppressed, failed artist who had only bit parts on the Dublin stage – and the decision is understandable. With the man's thespian activities in mind, it has to be said that Brian Marriner's perception in his book, *Missing Bodies*, that Ball played in a production of *Crime and Punishment* in 1935, and in that story, an old pawnbroker (a woman) is killed – by a young man wielding an axe.

CHAPTER 25

A Murderous Attack in Church
1948

'Most sacrilegious murder hath broke open
the Lord's anointed temple...'
SHAKESPEARE

Some cases of homicide are particularly complicated with the problem of finding out exactly what the circumstances are that led to a violent death. If we have a death in which two people struggled and grappled in extreme passion, with no-one else present, then everything in court is going to rest on exactly what went on and who did what. Today, with the modern sophisticated techniques of forensics applied to materials at the scene of crime, a detailed narrative of events leading to a death may be constructed with scientific support. But sixty years ago, when two women fought in a Dublin church, there was uncertainty as to exactly how the struggle resulted in a death.

The fight happened in the Glasnevin Church of Our Lady of the Seven Dolours. The church has now been replaced by a more modern building so again, we have to imagine the scene and its physical environment, but what happened was that Mary Gibbons, who was eighty-three years old and lived in Botanic Avenue, walked to church in August 1948, as she did every day. She walked through a warm summer day to the dark interior of the church and there she found a pew and began to pray. She was near the confessional, but was completely alone in the church – at least until the door opened again and someone else came in. The door closed after a beam of light had shot in momentarily.

Then we have another woman's story before we find out what happened in the church. Mary Daly was very hard up. Her landlady said that she was living at this time in lodgings with her husband and child, in Botanic Road. They had a struggle to find the weekly rent. Mary had been to beg money from a priest,

Our Lady of Seven Dolours, Glasnevin, today. The author

things were so bad, and he had given her the cash for the week's rent. But it was always going to be a constant battle to survive. In desperation, Mary went to the church in Glasnevin that day, but she had a hammer in her shopping bag. Her motives will always be a mystery, but the fact is that she went to the church with that potential murder weapon.

As Mary Gibbons prayed she was suddenly aware of a crack on her head. She was a large woman, well-built and still with some strength in spite of her age. After an initial sense of sheer stunned shock she turned to find Mary Daly, who was small and lightly made, wielding a hammer in the light of the church candle. One second she had been saying her Hail Marys and the next she was fighting for her life.

Mary grabbed Mary Daly's hand and the fight began. Mary Gibbons was bleeding profusely and she broke away and ran to the door of the church to cry for help but more hammer blows were slammed on her head. There was a trail of blood from the pew where the attack began, right to the door.

Some children came to church at that moment and they

heard the cries and screams inside, so they decided to run for help and at last, two adults came to try to help. A local butcher called James Canavan and a lorry driver, Thomas Mitchell, rushed to the church and they had to force open the door, as one woman was lodged against it. When they forced their way inside, Mitchell immediately realised he had to snatch the hammer from the smaller woman, and he did so, while Canavan tried to help the old lady in her pain. What happened then could have been the scene of any small-scale street brawl in Dublin – something not that uncommon. But it was the beginning of the confusion set before the forces of law in court, because a crowd had gathered, including the children, and what they saw and heard was not a hammer attack from behind but two women screaming, accusing each other of violence.

Old Mary Gibbons naturally told everyone that the younger woman had attacked her, but Daly then retorted with an accusation that Gibbons had tried to rob her and snatch her handbag. Detective Sergeant Joe Turner then arrived and that was the scene of noise and confusion he saw, and in a most unseemly place. An ambulance was called and Turner questioned Daly, who insisted that the old woman had tried to steal her bag. 'I was struggling with her to get my bag back!' she said.

As for Mary Gibbons, who was in hospital as Mary Daly was carried off to the police station, she was very seriously injured. Her skull had several wounds and bones were cracked; but she was able to give evidence in a special court held in the hospital of Mater Misericordiae in Eccles Street. It was to be a period of uncertainty for all concerned, mainly because the victim was confused about the actual events in the church. There was no confidence in her medical condition being either one thing or the other. At first, the doctors thought that she was pulling through and so when Daly stood before Judge O'Flynn on 16 August, the charge was wounding with intent, not attempted murder. But that was to change: at first the old lady was thought to be 'out of danger' but within a day she was dead. Back came Mary Daly to court to face a murder charge.

The trial was on 8 November at the Dublin Central Court. From the accused's home and family situation there came a motive, put together by the counsel for the prosecution, Sir John

Esmonde. The financial difficulties of the Daly family (with a young baby to support) meant that facts were uncovered that showed how desperate Mary Daly would be to get hold of some money; there had been a court order served on her to pay her rent. It was in the Church of the Seven Dolours that a priest had given her money just a short time before the attack, so it was an easy matter to find a motive in her return to that church in such dire straits. Was she carrying the hammer in case she had to extort money with threats this time, as opposed to begging and hoping for further largesse from the priest? That seemed to be the case.

The issue was, as there were no witnesses, whether or not Mary Daly went to the church with an intent to kill for money or whether there were other reasons for what she had in her bag that day. Testimony from the lorry driver who saw her that day and who restrained her, Mr Mitchell, was that Daly was distressed and excited, and that she did say that the hammer, which she had bought in Woolworth's store, was hers; similarly, the children in court, who heard the attack but did not see it, said that they did hear a voice saying 'Help… she's murdering me!' So who was doing the attacking?

Mary Daly was small and the older Mary Gibbons was tall and well-made; that was a factor that complicated things of course. Daly's defence argument was still that Gibbons had taken the hammer and attacked her; she may have been just five feet two tall and delicately made, but in the end, who had the clear motive? Why would the old lady have attacked Daly? The defence brought in a medical expert to say that the accused was so frail that she could not have used a hammer, and on the matter of her financial straits, Daly said that she did have £5 on her that day, and that the old lady was intending to steal that from her. The lengthy defence narrative was the familiar one of self-defence, creating a story in which Dalty, going into the church for quiet prayer and carrying her bag and purse, was attacked in the semi-darkness and that she happened to have the hammer with her and so she used it. That does not sit easily with the statement that she was too delicate to use a hammer.

The contradictions and confusions continued as Daly claimed that she had only at first hit Gibbons on the arm, that the old lady took the hammer and turned on her; being the stronger, she argued, the old lady then set about whacking her about the body with the weapon. She said, 'I tried to get out the door. I could not as the woman was leaning against it. I kept shouting for my husband for help. I thought I heard footsteps outside. I gave the woman another blow of the hammer on the head.. I did not know where I was hitting her. I hit her to get rid of her.'

The defence really dramatised this situation with great emotional emphasis, saying, 'Anyone who found themselves in Mrs Daly's position would probably have acted as she had done. There was no criminal intent.' But the judge pointed out that Mrs Gibbons had been praying and so that small as she was, Daly would have approached the old lady from a position above. That was a hypothetical detail that had some influence on the jury, who were out to deliberate for an hour or so and came back in with a guilty verdict, though they recommended mercy. But the sentence was one of hanging, with a date fixed in December that year.

The final chapter of this case is one of an incredible series of appeals; a date for appeal was set and then everything depended on points of law, mainly that the deceased had made a formal 'dying declaration' regarding the attack (at that time only one of minor assault of course) and that such a matter could not be admissible in a murder trial. In an example of what must have been a desperately stressful situation, the judges rejected this but then opened up the possibility of a final appeal to the Supreme Court. There was then a complete re-trial because of legal technicalities, and again the judgement was guilty of murder. For a second time Mary Daly stood in court and heard her death sentence. But the string of frustrating and dramatic trials ended there, as shortly after that second decision her sentence was commuted to life imprisonment. Mary did a seven-year stretch, followed by time with a religious order, and then went back into her life.

Only very rarely in criminal trials has there been such doubt and uncertainty about the actual events of a case, and the fact that so many people arrived on the scene just a little too late to have any definite evidence on the series of events in the fight only served to make the trial more complex.

CHAPTER 26

The Mohangi Case
1963

*'When police searched the premises, they found seventeen
bodily parts in the storeroom...'*
GEOFF TIBBALLS

Shan Mohangi did not want the fire brigade on his Harcourt Street premises in August 1963, in spite of the fact that there was smoke pouring out of the place and he had already had to open the door to a young couple passing by who knocked and aroused him to ask if help was needed. He even told the fire chief that there was nothing to worry about and wanted the engines to go away. But they had shot there at high speed from Tara Street and Captain Michael Grey knew that there was a serious fire there where Mohangi stood, apparently complacent. It was to be the beginning of what has become known as the 'Green Tureen Case'.

Mohangi took Grey down to a basement to show him the cause of all the black smoke: there were some rags of cloth on a grill, and Grey quite rightly wanted to speak to someone in authority. But the manager of the restaurant was not there. Firemen were taking no chances and were about to put some water into the back area of the cellar when Mohangi stood in their way, saying that there was only a storeroom through there. We have to feel for poor Captain Grey, who finally had to be content with a warning and a rather low-key exit from what had clearly looked like a severely dangerous situation. The young Indian Mohangi, who said he was a medical student, had been behaving most peculiarly.

That evening there was to be a dinner there in Harcourt Street at the restaurant, and a man called Desmond Mullen from Shankill, was to be there, with his young sister Hazel. He arrived that afternoon after all the drama and listened again to Mohangi's explanation for the smell of burning, as another man had done also, a student who came. Mohangi said that Hazel would not be coming to join them.

Mohangi and the Mullens had become friendly about a year before these events; Mohangi was twenty-three and Hazel just fifteen when they began walking out together. Mohangi was Indian, and from Natal. In 1961 he came to Dublin to study medicine at the Royal College of Surgeons, and in the old tradition of students everywhere, he was working to pay fees and subsistence costs. The young peoples' relationship deepened and Mohangi had asked Hazel to marry him, but Mrs Mullen sensibly advised caution and there was a postponement.

On the fateful day when Hazel did not arrive for the dinner, Mullen and his girlfriend ate dinner and then went out for the night, expecting Hazel to turn up, but she did not. Mrs Mullen was understandably very worried and Mohangi tried to stall her with excuses and fantasies. He spun a yarn, saying that the girl had rung him from the Bank of Ireland, cancelling their day together. But there had been no word from her at home. Mrs Mullen said she was distraught. Mullen and Mohangi went to the Mullen home and the medical student started to project his performance of 'worried boyfriend' to the world.

The police had to be told, as she was now unaccountably missing. Constable Donaghue was on the case and he took details of her supposed last statements and movements, as far as these were known. Later, at trial, Mohangi said, 'She had no other boyfriends… We were in love and planned to be married. She must have been kidnapped from the streets and she is being held prisoner somewhere. You must find her before something terrible happens.' After that, as more time passed and the level of concern increased, Mohangi accelerated the act of worried and tense lover, going out to search all the places he thought she might be found –places he of course would know from their time together. By the Sunday, the matter was urgent and a Detective Inspector was on the case – Matthew Kennedy. The detective, knowing that nothing had been found and that there had been no sighting of the girl, did the obvious thing – just as had been done in the case of Dr Crippen many years before – he suggested that they search the flat in Harcourt Street. Mohangi naturally protested, and that was a mistake.

The turning-point came after that first fruitless search, because Kennedy found out about the fire alarm, and more importantly, he found out about Mohangi being seen by a neighbour walking up the stairs with 'an Irish girl'. Someone said that the girl had left alone at about midnight. There was a stepping-up of enquiries about Hazel then; officers questioned people who knew her and there were plans for a more thorough search of the rooms in Harcourt Street. An odd thing then happened, something that directed attention away from the immediate area; a family friend of the Mullens said he was sure that Hazel was walking around the Crumlin area, somehow out of touch and mentally troubled. When this came to nothing, after a long period of walking around with Hazel's picture, the family were understandably in despair.

But the Harcourt Street premises were to become the focus of intense police activity after a cook turned up for work and was subject to a noxious smell; she found some bones wrapped in newspaper and took them out to the bin, but still there was a stink. Suspicions were aroused, and people began to feel that it was strange that the young student would not go to the police regarding the fire and now the smell and the bones down in the cellars. By Wednesday, the police were in Harcourt Street again and there they found Mohangi lying in bed with a gas heater blasting gas at him, and a bottle of tablets by his bed. There was a suicide note saying, 'Everything belonging to me goes to Maureen Kelly.' He was taken to hospital, and the search of the premises began in earnest.

Superintendents McShane and McLoughlin had the unpleasant task of searching for materials in the midst of an overpowering smell. When they came across what was almost certainly a human thigh bone, the net was definitely closing in on Shan Mohangi, who was recovering consciousness in hospital. Altogether, the hunt in the cellar resulted in seventeen body parts being found; it was now a job for a pathologist and Dr Maurice Hickey came, to confirm that what they had there was a case of the dismemberment of a young girl – done with a meat cleaver and by someone with the medical knowledge needed to do that task effectively. The scenario became as gruesome as anything from Rillington Place; bits of flesh were found behind a heater; bloodstained garments turned up, and then personal belongings, all adding up to the fact that Hazel Mullen had been murdered there, and then a most horrific act of butchering had taken place.

It was all up for Mohangi; discharged from hospital, he was escorted to gaol and the two detectives who had experienced the foul effects of the man's murderous handiwork talked to him there. The student said that the crisis came when Hazel had told him she had kissed another man. This led to his account of how, among his own people at home, chastity was paramount when wedding was discussed, and that as he had learned that Hazel was a virgin, he was more determined than ever to marry her and that she should be chaste. When she said that she had kissed another, Mohangi told the officers that he did not know what had happened to him. 'I had always loved and worshipped her for that one thing. I was in a rage at the time. I caught hold of her and put my arms around her neck...'

He said he had panicked and that the death was accidental. But of course he had known what to do to try to hide her body: he said he had been burning body parts and dissecting the girl when the firemen had come. He had had to leave the horrible work unfinished while he played the part of worried lover and then actually gone back to the cutting and burning on the Monday. It was then that the suicide was discussed and it was ascertained that the Maureen Kelly he had written about was his first friend in the city; she was found and questioned and it was soon explained that they had been close friends. She was a nurse, young and pretty, and they had always been close and that she had been at the flat just a day before Hazel had been killed.

There was no body part to be available so that doctors could either confirm or deny the supposed fact that Mohangi had cut Hazel's throat, but there was clearly a case of murder – intended, premeditated and ruthless. The trial began in February 1964. It was a case of there being a large medical presence in court: expert witnesses were needed to clarify the probable cause of death because if Hazel had been strangled purposefully and then cut and burned, that was a very different thing from an accidental death which might have happened in a situation of intimacy. One doctor said that a sudden and even unintentional pressure on the throat could cause a stoppage of the heart.

The crux of the matter was the attitude of Mohangi to Hazel.

He had written a letter to her just a day before her death, passionate and loving, saying, 'There never will be a heart so true/ for I am devoted to you, my love/ and forever will be true /I love you my Hazel.' But of course, with all the revolting detail of the dismemberment and blood, with the odour of burning body-parts filling Harcourt Street, it was hard for anyone to allow thoughts of the accused being anything but a savage. If, however, the death had been caused by what one lawyer called 'playful inhibition' then it was a matter of manslaughter, in spite of all the gore and revulsion involved. But after three hours, the verdict was that Mohangi was guilty of murder and he had nothing to say to the court before the death sentence was passed on him.

But the scaffold did not wait for him; there was an appeal and on that occasion, he was found to be guilty of aggravated manslaughter. This would be therefore 'involuntary' – that is to say, committed while the person was doing a dangerous or reckless act. He was given a sentence of seven years' penal servitude.

Horror and Farce

D ublin can arguably lay claim to one of the most foul and repulsive killings in the annals of murder. This happened in 1717 and a report on a chapbook printed in Edinburgh gives the details in the most explicit form:

> *There was lately a fellow in Dublin called Charles Lovegrive, apothecary from Germany, who, seeing his bedfellow the skipper of a small vessel receive some gold and money, killed him when he was asleep; and to conceal the murder, he cut off his head from his shoulders, and burned his skull in the fire, quartered and divided him into pieces, and at several times carried him to the waterside, and threw him in at Essex Quay... The like may warn people of all ranks to guard against bad fellowship...*

Such grisly tales are the staple material of crime casebooks, and are common in all modern cities, but in Dublin we have some examples from the records that show with acute and powerful human experience both ends of the spectrum of crime. Two examples of this will make a fitting coda to this collection of stories.

The first is a tale of the two Bridgets: in March 1821, a young woman who was living in the home of a Captain Peck in Portland Place near Mountjoy Square was murdered. Apparently, a girl called out to her that the Captain had had an accident and that he wanted the girl to take his greatcoat to him. When the girl did so, she returned to find the house ransacked, and there had been no accident but her mistress had been killed. It took no time at all to find and arrest two Bridgets – Ennis and Butterly.

They had killed Miss Thompson, and there was a back-story to the case, as Bridget Ennis told people in gaol. The report states that she had had an intimacy with the Captain while employed by him. The Bridgets had then planned to run away to England and needed funds. Robbing the Captain's house was to find some cash for that purpose, but the girls murdered Miss Thompson. Butterly testified: 'I had dragged Miss Thompson two or three steps down before Ennis had left the house but had not given her a blow or other injury at that time; I pushed her down the stairs until I got her into the kitchen. I then seized a poker and began to beat her...'

It all led to the gallows. It was a case as common as drinking tea. The criminal law machine ground on, with the desperate underclass as the fodder, pushed to extreme savagery by their poverty and disenchantment and envy as they saw the very rich walk around in a world of the poverty of the masses.

On the other hand, just thirty years later we have the case of Vladimir Pecherin, working at the time for the Redemptorist mission in Dublin. By the side of the previous case, this is bizarre. In 1855, Pecherin was preaching in Kingstown (Dun Laoghaire). On 5 November he took part in the burning of some 'immoral literature'. But it appears that a local Protestant clergyman ordered a boy to throw a Bible on the pyre and it was soon made known what Pecherin had done. He went to trial in Green Street (where Newgate had stood). The whole business was such a farce that at one point in the examinations we have this interchange:

Mr Curran: *How do you know it was a testament you saw?*
Witness: *I saw the word 'testament' on the book.*
Mr Curran: *Was it a new or an old testament?*
Witness: *It was newly bound.*

Pecherin was acquitted and the general populace of the city were very much on his side. His body was buried in Glasnevin but has since been exhumed and lies elsewhere, on the orders of the Redemptorists, according to writer Zonovy Zinik.

Such are the vagaries and ironies of the history of crime, and crime in Dublin has always given us stories of wonder, farce and sheer high level drama and sensation.

Images of the sharp contrasts of the city: McDaid's *pub where writers gathered,
including Behan and Kavanagh – and the pub opposite the Castle with images of
national heroes.* The author

Bibliography

1 Books

Behan, Brendan, *The Quare Fellow*, in *Complete Plays*, Methuen, 1978

Carey, Tim, *Mountjoy: The Story of a Prison*, Collins Press, 2000

Craig, Maurice, *Dublin 1660-1860*, Liberties Press, 2006

Donnelly, James S and Miller, Kerby, *Irish Popular Culture 1650-1850*, Irish Academic Press, 1998

Ellmann, Richard, *Oscar Wilde*, Hamish Hamilton, 1997

Fielding, Steve, *Pierrepoint: A Family of Executioners*, Blake, 2006

Fielding, Steve, *The Hangman's Record Vol. 1 1866-1899*, Chancery House Press, 1999

Greene, David H and Stephens, *Edmund M J M Synge 1871-1909*, Collier Books, 1961

Griffin, Brian, *Sources for the Study of Crime in Ireland 1801-1921*, Four Courts Press, 2005

Harris, Frank, *Oscar Wilde: His Trials and Confessions*, Macmillan, 1912

Hickey, D J and Doherty J E, *A New Dictionary of Irish History from 1800*, Gill and Macmillan, 2003

Government of Ireland: *Dublin Castle at the Heart of Irish History*, 2nd edition, 2004

Hopkins, Frank, *Rare Old Dublin: Heroes, Hawkers and Hoors*, Mercier, 2002

Kee, Robert, *The Bold Fenian Men*, Penguin, 1972

Kelly, James, *Gallows Speeches from Eighteenth Century Ireland*, Four Courts Press, 2001

Kiernan, V G, *The Duel in European History*, Oxford University Press, 1988

Lecky, W E H, *A History of Ireland in the Eighteenth Century*, Longmans Green, 1892

Le Fanu, W R, *Seventy years of Irish Life*, Kessinger Publishing, 2007

McCarthy, Michael J F, *Five Years in Ireland 1895-1900*,
      Hodges Figgis, 1901
Marriner, Brian, *Missing Bodies*, Arrow Books, 1994
Marshall, Peter, *Mother Leakey and the Bishop*, Oxford
      University Press, 2007
Pakenham, Thomas and Valerie, *A Traveller's Companion to
      Dublin*, Robinson, 2003
Palmer, Stanley H, *Police and Protest in England and Ireland
      1750-1850*, Cambridge University Press, 1988
Somerville-Large, Peter, *Dublin*, Hamish Hamilton, 1979
Stanley, Derek, *North Dublin From the Liffey to Balbriggan*,
      Nonsuch, 2006
Tibballs, Geoff, *The Murder Guide to Great Britain*, Boxtree,
      1994
Townshend, Charles, *Easter 1916: The Irish Rebellion*, Penguin,
      2005
Wilkinson, George Theodore, *The Newgate Calendar*, Sphere,
      1991

2 Articles

'Classic Irish Cases' in *True Crime*, July, 2007, pp.8 -12
Garnham, Neal, 'The Trials of James Cutter and Henry Baron
      Santry: two cases in the administration of criminal justice in
      early eighteenth century Ireland,' in *Irish Historical Studies*,
      Vol. XXXI, No.123,1998-9, pp. 328-342
Murphy, Sean J, *Irish Historical Mysteries*, eircom.net
Pierse, Michael, 'The Miracle of Monto?' in *An Phoblacht*,
      Sept 2002
Powell, Martin J, 'Political Toasting in Eighteenth Century
      Ireland' in *History*, Vol. 91, No. 4, Oct 2006, pp. 508-529
Rowan, Archibald Hamilton, *Memoirs*
Sanders, John, 'Murder Beneath the Altar' in *True Detective*,
      Winter, 2006, pp.75-+78
Zink, Zinovy, 'Freelance', in *Times Literary Supplement*, 9 Nov
      2007

3 Journals and original reports

American Historical Review
Annual Register, 1821
Dublin Penny Journal, No.18 Vol. 1, Oct 27, 1832

Dublin Review, XL, March, 1856
Gentleman's Magazine,1857: Sylvanus Urban
The Graphic, 1878
Kilmainham, the Bastille of Ireland, Kilmainham Jail Restoration
   Society, 1982
Notes and Queries
Trial of James Spollen for the Murder of Mr George Samuel Little,
   Dublin: Edward J Milliken, 1857

4 Archives
Record 4666 Directory of Sources for Women's History in
   Ireland
National Archives of Ireland, Supreme Court and Court of
   Criminal Appeal Records
National Library of Ireland: *The Past from the Press,* historical
   documents file
Official Account of the Trial of Lord Santry, from
   www.chaptersofdublin.com/General
Proceedings of the Old Bailey at
   www.oldbaileyonline.org/history/crime/verdicts
The Times Digital Archive

5 Websites
www.arts.guardian.co.uk/curtainup/story
www.geocities.com/richard.clark32@btinternet.com/eire
www.nationalarchives.ie/tpics/crown_jewels/index
www.newryjournal.co.uk
www.nls.uk/resources

TRUE CRIME FROM WHARNCLIFFE

Foul Deeds and Suspicious Deaths Series

Barking, Dagenham & Chadwell Heath
Barnsley
Bath
Bedford
Birmingham
Black Country
Blackburn and Hyndburn
Bolton
Bradford
Brighton
Bristol
Cambridge
Carlisle
Chesterfield
Colchester
Coventry
Croydon
Cumbria
Derby
Dublin
Durham
Ealing
Folkestone and Dover
Grimsby
Guernsey
Guildford
Halifax
Hampstead, Holborn and St Pancras
Huddersfield
Hull

Leeds
Leicester
Lewisham and Deptford
Liverpool
London's East End
London's West End
Manchester
Mansfield
More Foul Deeds Birmingham
More Foul Deeds Chesterfield
More Foul Deeds Wakefield
Newcastle
Newport
Norfolk
Northampton
Nottingham
Oxfordshire
Pontefract and Castleford
Portsmouth
Rotherham
Scunthorpe
Southend-on-Sea
Southport
Staffordshire and The Potteries
Stratford and South Warwickshire
Tees
Warwickshire
Wigan
York

OTHER TRUE CRIME BOOKS FROM WHARNCLIFFE

A-Z of Yorkshire Murder
Black Barnsley
Brighton Crime and Vice 1800-2000
Durham Executions
Essex Murders
Executions & Hangings in Newcastle
  and Morpeth
Norfolk Mayhem and Murder

Norwich Murders
Strangeways Hanged
The A-Z of London Murders
Unsolved Murders in Victorian and
  Edwardian London
Unsolved Norfolk Murders
Unsolved Yorkshire Murders
Yorkshire's Murderous Women

Please contact us via any of the methods below for more information or a catalogue.

WHARNCLIFFE BOOKS

47 Church Street – Barnsley – South Yorkshire – S70 2AS
Tel: 01226 734555 – 734222 Fax: 01226 – 734438
E-mail: enquiries@pen-and-sword.co.uk
Website: www.wharncliffebooks.co.uk

Index

Spollen, Mary 82-4
Stafford, peter 94-5
Stanley, Sir Edward 49
Stanyhurst, Richard 3
Stevens, James 21-22
Synge, John 4, 106-9

Taylor, Dr 78
Touchet, Mervyn 11
Tone, Wolfe 47, 59
Travers, Mary 86-9
Turpin, Dick 5

Vance, Sheriff 60-2
Vane, Francis Fletcher 138-9
Vicker, Sir Arthur 112-5

Wade, Peter 99-101
Wall, Charles 38
Walsh, J E 56
Walsh, Martin 101
Wam, Richard 27
Wandesford, Sir Christopher 12-14
Weeks, James Eyre 62
Wentworth, Thomas 11, 15
White, Jack 125
Wilde, Jane 86-9
Wilde, Oscar 2, 10
Wilde, Sir William 4, 86-8
Wilson, John 132
Worsdale, James 42
Wright, Arnold 119

Yeats, W B 1, 106-7, 110, 111

Zinik, Zinovy 161

Places

Abbey Theatre 106-9
Antrim 16
Aran Islands 107
Arbour Hill gaol 134
Athenry 7
Aungier Street 34, 127

Baggott Street 64
Ballygar 143
Ballymena 16
Belfast 4, 53
Benburb 6
Bible and Sun 27
Black Dog (gaol) 3
Black Lane 59
Blackrock Felons' Association 55
Booterstown 145
Botanic Road 150

Bradogue, river 83
Brary 87
Broadstone terminus 80-1
Bull Lane 97

Canterbury 117
Capel Street 16, 67
Castle Street 25
Central Criminal Court 143
Chamber Street 37
Chancery lane Bridewell 126
Cherry Lane 66
Christ Church 12
Clonmel Assizes 46
Clonskeagh Road 114
Clontarf Wood 47
College Green 41, 126
Coombe 33
Coombe Lying-In Hospital 66
Cork 4, 71
Corn market 3, 125

Dame Street 21
Dawson Street 51
Dublin Castle 14, 66, 96, 112-6
Dublin District Court 148, 152
Dublin House of Commons 42
Dublin United Tramway Company 122
Dun Laoghaire 161

Eccles Street 152

Fishamble Street 52
Four Courts 3

General Post Office 125
Glasgow 121
Glasnevin 75, 150
Goldsmith Street 131
Grangegorman penitentiary 3
Great Britain Street 66
Great george's Street 140
Green Street 17, 38, 92, 161
Green Street Commission Court 99

Hammond Lane 44
Harcourt Street 155-6
Howth 71-2

Ireland's Eye 72
Irish Sea 80

Kerry 117, 118
Kilmainham 3, 59, 66, 68, 94, 100-1
Kilmainham Common 40
Kilmainham District Court 143
King's Bench 14
Kingstown 161